# God's Words of the Day:

## A Guide to Identity, Faith, and Deliverance

STEPHEN LEFEBVRE

# CONTENTS

"Truth is finite within the process of cause and effect, not fluid. There is one truth in the universe: everything that happened simply happened; everything that exists simply exists. Our understanding of it or lack thereof does not change its existence. Our understanding of truth will lead us to Christ."
– Stephen Lefebvre

# INTRODUCTION

The table of contents is vast in this work for a reason. In the process of about 60 days (inside and outside of a 42-day media-fasting period right in the beginning of the Covid-19 pandemic), God taught me and my church family a large number of subjects, each of which could be its own book. The goal of why I'm writing this in the first place is not to write tons of books and become a famous author. I hope my name is forgotten in a multitude of names if it means that Christ is remembered forever.

This book is for everyone who is hungry for knowledge and truth in Christ. If you're not hungry for knowledge and truth in Christ, KEEP READING ANYWAY! I'm absolutely certain that God has placed a calling on my life to reach lukewarm Christians. I've lived and experienced being a lukewarm Christian before, but I have also experienced what it means to be completely blown away by revelations of truth and fire in the Holy Spirit. The Holy Spirit led me to write down these "Words of the Day" which outline everything as a whole of what it means to have identity in Christ. You will not live lukewarm after applying these teachings to your life! These words of the day were revealed through every-day experiences, through words in people's testimonies, sermons that were "coincidentally" shared to me, and very specifically reinforced by passages in the Bible. Along with the list of words, God inspired me to write specific sermons/guides on subject points about faith, affirmations, and being delivered from demonic influence and mindsets. For future reference in this book, Bible references I use will almost always come from the Authorized King James Version Bible, unless otherwise stated. The KJV may be my favorite version, but I'm also a firm believer that God can use literally anything to talk to us and teach us his truths. He has talked to my spirit directly before. I've seen patterns of numbers that remind me of passages in the Bible to go check out and read again. I've felt urges to go to places, speak to people, help certain people at certain times, et cetera, and God has been so faithful to teach me in those situations! He even taught me a valuable lesson through my interaction with a stinkbug. So, again, he teaches through ANYTHING!

This book would have been a lot longer if I had included the full story of how God inspired the Umbrella-Belief Meeting (this is a pseudo name for the real church group) to perform a media-fast during Lent. I've tried reaching out to about 10 people to find out their understanding of the event that took place because I was unfortunately not present at that particular meeting. Maybe it was for the best so that my perception would not get in the way of what God wanted to teach thereafter. When I finally receive all the stories, maybe that will be a separate piece altogether. In the meantime, this is the basis of how the story occurred:

The Umbrella-Belief Meeting is a church that operates right out of what the book of Acts describes the early church to be. We ARE the church, spreading God's love to others through relationship with the Holy Spirit, meeting at individuals' houses, sharing communion, worshipping, and teaching each other equally through the scriptures, as God reveals their truths, and through experiences as God pours out his Spirit into our lives. One Friday night during a meeting, a couple of newcomers, a mother and her 20-year-old daughter, had joined upon referral of a close friend who was concerned for the daughter's spiritual safety. I've asked her before writing this if she would like her name in the book or a pseudo name. So, from now on, I'll reference her as "Angel." Angel has had a difficult life with various traumas, some subtle and some extreme. Come to find out that these traumas created opportunities to invite demons to manifest through her body, and that night during the meeting was no exception. From what I have already gathered from those who've responded to my inquiries about the story, after a time of worship and communion (which is just regular eating of food that everyone brought, when we take time to remember Christ and give thanks for his sacrifice), Angel and the close friend were talking to our pastor, Linda. He asked Linda to pray for Angel because she was constantly being afflicted by evil spirits. It's common for us to pray for each other; we fervently believe in God's healing power and have seen diverse miracles of healings take place before our eyes. God had been growing us as a church family for a long time, but what was about to unfold was something unlike the Umbrella-Belief Meeting had ever experienced before! The following is the best rendition of the experience that I can describe with what has been told to me:

Linda began to pray. Angel's eyes rolled back as she started to bend forward in what looked like horrible pain coming from her midsection. Her soft, timid voice became gargled and raspy. She let out a scream as if Linda's prayers were arrows; Linda decided to change tone of authority once she realized what was happening to her. Once Angel started to noticeably manifest, about ten out of the thirty in attendance were comfortable enough to join in prayer, laying hands on her. Some prayed in tongues. Others were specifically trying to call out the demon to leave her body. Others believed in authority that they could ask questions and get answers. Some questions asked were as follows: "How many demons are inside? What's your name?" Angel's voice sounded high-pitched at points with hisses in between statements. She said, "There are FOURTY of us in here!" and, "I am a lying spirit. I lie. I tell the truth too, but I lie!" The demons' confidence was starting to build as onlookers developed fear of the situation, having never experienced anything like this before, some being newer to the faith than others. The demons were flinging accusations in between the pain, as if they knew people's impurities. One person thought Angel was faking the whole thing. Another onlooker described the situation like that of what happens in movies but that her head didn't turn all the way around. A police officer patrolling the neighborhood knocked on the door to ask about the parking situation outside. He asked, "What's happening here?" The person who opened the door said, "We're just having a church meeting." As Angel was screaming and swearing while everyone continued to pray, the officer said, "This doesn't look like church to me..." He hurried away, adding this event to his list of "I thought I've seen everything on Friday nights." This whole event took about three hours before Angel was able to calm down and manifest herself instead of demons. For those members who had been there, that night will forever be engraved in their hearts and minds. Concerning the validity of all the facts of this story as a whole, I would hope that if there are any missing pieces, that my church family reading this would fill me in on the complete story eventually.

Three consecutive Fridays passed, and Angel had been brought to each of those Umbrella-Belief Meetings to have more demons cast out of her. The deliverances took place in the basement with way fewer people while everyone else proceeded with meetings upstairs, still being able to hear her screams. A select few decided to leave the group because they couldn't emotionally handle what meetings were becoming. Passionately seeking guidance from the

Holy Spirit on what was to be our next step, Linda received an understanding that we were to go through a fasting period in order for the Umbrella-Belief Meeting to gain wisdom and knowledge about how to perform deliverances correctly. As a group, we were to abstain from all distractions from social media as well as from movies and secular music, replacing those things with prayer and communion with the Holy Spirit. Although I had not experienced the original event, I was eager to come alongside my church family and support them during what I call "the Fast," and I was eager to see God do something new in my life because of it as well! From March 1st to April 12, 2020, most of us who were passionate about being empowered in the Spirit were on board with a media fast. Some did actual fasting of food as well. Everyone's fast was slightly different, based on what God wanted us to push aside for that time being. We even created a separate group on Sundays for those of us who wanted to converge and ask God questions together, studying the Word, inviting individuals who specifically had deliverance ministries to join us via video calls to teach us what they know.

The whole forty-two days of various fasting ended with a Jewish seder and many of the Umbrella-Belief Meeting members standing outside their houses on Easter Sunday, speaking out a contractual declaration speech to God and a blessing over our region and country, of which I had the honor of proofreading and editing the day before. So, for myself, the speech was fresh on my mind, and I think that had an effect on my mindset when I woke up that Sunday. This feeling came over me as I woke up; I felt God say to me, "DON'T DRINK COFFEE!" much like how a father tells his toddler not to play with the electrical socket, pointing his finger out like the toddler is in trouble. Suffice to say, I was surprised. I agreed, had two days of headaches, and I haven't had coffee since. Remembering how God spoke to my spirit about it empowered me to stop my addiction, which I discovered was an idol in my life and a gateway to maintaining an addictive personality concerning other vices. God was calling me to have NO distractions, although he was gracious enough to let me drink coffee during the Fast. During the Fast, he was giving me urges to write certain keywords down as I encountered them. Each word popped out at me, along with a definition or story of what God wanted me to learn about them, each backed up by scripture and a strange process of logic that I didn't know I possessed. It's important to note that three months before Angel ever visited the Umbrella-Belief Meeting, a prophetic pastor prophesied over my life when I visited a different church, stating that I would have an ability to read God's Word and have an understanding unlike most other people in my circle. At that point, I had not been consistent in my daily devotional studies and only started journaling in January, but God made this prophecy come true during the Fast. I have firsthand experience on what it's like to be truly inspired by God to write his words, and I am exceedingly humbled.

Even as I write this introduction, God has been influencing my words and reminding me of why he gave me this information in the order that he did. The Words of the Day all sum up a Christian's identity and reason for existence, focused and centered on Christ. The sermon on faith is to teach what is required in order to adopt the Words of the Day. The affirmations prayer list and the extensive list of demons that are attracted to specific mindsets are used in delivering Christians from evil mindsets of their pasts while teaching them how to daily and consistently renew their minds towards the obedience of Christ. When it comes to the specific subject of demons, like Angel had been suffering, if one is not a Christian who specifically closes the door points of what's inviting demons, demons that are cast out or away from a person could decide to come back stronger with more help from other demons. So, it's imperative to have belief in Christ as the cornerstone of all daily renewal of the mind and deliverance from demonic influences in order to close door points. It's important to understand salvation through the gospel. Without it, demons have rights to stick around you and affect your life. Don't be afraid! What a wonderful friend we have in Jesus who HEALS and DELIVERS us from the devil! Please enjoy the following truths in God's Word.

# CHAPTER ONE: RESPONSIBILITY

"It is not my responsibility to fix other people. It is God who works the works into every person's heart."

The quote above was all I mentioned in my journal about this Word of the Day. In fact, many of the words have small explanations on which I will need to expound upon after the quotes.

Jeremiah 17:10 says, "I the LORD search the heart, I try the reins, even to give every man according to his ways, and according to the fruit of his doings." There are many verses in the Bible that show just how involved God is inside our hearts, our emotions, and our minds. He knows the hearts of men and gives them according to what they do with what's in their hearts. Pharaoh had enmity towards the Hebrew people. When Moses told Pharaoh to let the people go, on multiple occasions God "hardened his heart" so that he would refuse. He already possessed that pride to say No, and God amplified what was there so that God would be glorified after all the marvels of the plagues, freeing his people, and decimating the Egyptian forces.

The logic behind the original quote stems from the understanding of the nature of our hearts. No matter how much one can share his heart to others through words and actions, one's heart is still his own. God did not give each person the choice to be born or to choose WHAT life is, but he gave each one of us the ability to choose life through Jesus Christ's sacrifice and resurrection or to choose death by denying Christ. It is an individual's choice, not our choice for others. I cannot be a good Christian for you, nor can you be one for me. When you possess something that is specifically your own, you are the sole proprietor of how that is used in your life; this includes what you choose to believe.

What does this say about our responsibility as believers in Jesus Christ? We have the Great Commission in Matthew 28:16-20. It is our responsibility to go out into all the world, teaching everyone we can about everything that Christ taught, specifically the significance of his death and resurrection, and receiving the Holy Spirit. So, the most attractive habit Christians tend to create is that WE are the ones who make others convert with what we preach, as if WE are the ones winning souls instead of the Holy Spirit through us. With this mindset, it is very easy to attach our view of personal value as Christians based on whether people choose death instead of life. Do not be discouraged about your own self-worth if someone else chooses not to believe what you preach about Christ. Also, don't make your Christian walk ALL ABOUT MAKING others find Jesus. Just live in the joy that you are saved, and hopefully God will be able to convince others by the fruit of what he multiplies from inside your heart. God does the work in their hearts. We are just his hands, feet, and vessels.

# CHAPTER TWO: DISCIPLESHIP

"Most people think this is all about serving God, but he is telling me otherwise. In fact, God doesn't need our help in order to do anything! Being the disciple that he wants you to be means that you are simply called to seek his identity, seek his will diligently, and to BE his heart. Being his heart makes service flow naturally."

Just like I had written about "RESPONSIBILITY," "DISCIPLESHIP" is a term of identity in Christ that is way more than we can ever DO as mere mortals in our own power. Discipleship in this case is the action of understanding what our responsibilities are as Christians in that it is all about BEING Christ's character so that we may do and follow God's will in other people's lives. It's not about doing in our own power what we think is God's will for others so that we can attain Christ's character. From my perspective, it seems that those who are only focused on doing things for God in their own power are just like the lukewarm Christians described in Matthew 7:22-23 of whom hypothetically said to Jesus, "Lord, Lord, haven't we" done all this great stuff in your name? And he'll say, "I never knew you!" Lukewarm Christians are not focused on KNOWING God, and they are too mindful of the things of the flesh. (Refer to Romans chapter 8 about the ways of the flesh and the Spirit.)

Being a disciple, we must let the Holy Spirit lead us in everything we do, as Romans 8:14 says, "For as many as are led by the Spirit of God, they are the sons of God." This mirrors what Christ says in John 14:26, describing the Holy Spirit. "But the Comforter, which is the Holy Ghost, whom the Father will send in my name, he shall teach you all things, and bring all things to your remembrance, whatsoever I have said unto you." He even helps us pray! Romans 8:26, "Likewise the Spirit also helpeth our infirmities: for we know not what we should pray for as we ought: but the Spirit itself maketh intercession for us with groanings which cannot be uttered." (Those two verses will be repeated a lot in future chapters.) Just as the disciples followed every intercession that Christ spoke into their lives, so must we follow the leading of the Holy Spirit.

Ted Shuttlesworth Jr. says it very plainly in one of his popular Christian podcasts and in his book, *A Complete Guide to Biblical Fasting*[1]: "A disciple emulates the disciplines of his master."

We are to emulate Jesus Christ as the ultimate example of self-discipline. Everything Christ ever did was centered around knowing the Father, being who his Father called him to be, and saying/doing what the Father wanted.

# CHAPTER THREE: DEVOTION

"God wants our faith to lead to undistracted choosing to follow God's law of love and BECOMING his heart and desiring his purity in everything we are. Organize your life in sections and ask God how you can live that portion of your life in the purity of devotion he desires so that you do not make God jealous for you."

There is a plethora of verses and stories all over the Bible about God being a jealous God. Who else deserves all our praise? How many times did Israel have to learn the same lesson over and over again, that there is no other God but Yahuah, Adonai, Elohim? It doesn't matter how many of his names you know, as long as he is the only God in your life. God reminded Israel through his law that there are no other gods besides him. Exodus 20:2-6 says, "I am the LORD thy God, which have brought thee out of the land of Egypt, out of the house of bondage. Thou shalt have no other gods before me. Thou shalt not make unto thee any graven image, or any likeness of any thing that is in heaven above, or that is in the earth beneath, or that is in the water under the earth. Thou shalt not bow down thyself to them, nor serve them: for I the LORD thy God am a jealous God, visiting the iniquity of the fathers upon the children unto the third and fourth generation of them that hate me; And showing mercy unto thousands of them that love me, and keep my commandments."

If you didn't catch that explanation at the end, God is clearly saying that those who worship anything else besides him actually hate him, and those who follow his commandments love him. In the Old and New Testaments, God's law does not change; how it is implemented in our lives is subject to further debate and study between those who believe that the law is abolished or lasts forever. We will touch upon the law later. The point is that WHATEVER God wants YOU to do will show that you love him when you follow his commands. I love God, so I listened to his command, for example, when he told me to stop drinking coffee.

Luke 16:13 says, "No servant can serve two masters: for either he will hate the one, and love the other; or else he will hold to the one, and despise the other. Ye cannot serve God and mammon." We can look at it in this way: saying "maybe" to God is equivalent to saying "no for now," and when you pass from this world having said "no" to God (specifically concerning believing in Christ), you will be wasted.

All lukewarm Christians serve themselves first before they serve the Father, in turn not truly serving him fully at all. Do not take this as an opportunity to condemn yourself. Jesus "was not sent to condemn the world but to save the world through him." (John 3:17) Take this as an opportunity to know that reading further is imperative to the health of your soul!

# CHAPTER FOUR: PATIENCE

"Patience happens when your beliefs are tested. Patience is the opposite of what results when you're anxious, of which anxiety is a derivative of fear. Patience is a peace in God's promises that you know are true in faith, and it empowers you. James 1:2-3 says, 'Count it all joy when ye fall into divers temptations; knowing this, that the trying of your faith worketh patience.' Each instance of your beliefs being challenged is another opportunity to remember what God says is truth. The way to battle temptations and win is to declare to God what you know is his truth and promises, and he will quicken your heart."

Philippians 4:6-7 says, "Be careful for nothing; but in every thing by prayer and supplication with thanksgiving let your requests be made known unto God. And the peace of God, which passeth all understanding, shall keep your hearts and minds through Christ Jesus." These verses reveal that the truth of Christ in our hearts and minds is what gives us peace. Peace is the emotional state of patience. There's a reason why Jesus says in Matthew 11:29-30, "Take my yoke upon you, and learn of me; for I am meek and lowly in heart: and ye shall find rest unto your souls. For my yoke is easy, and my burden is light." For those who don't know, a yoke is a device that rests on the shoulders of an animal that pulls carriages or tilling tools in gardening. That animal's burden is extremely heavy, but when we put on Christ, our souls are uplifted because of the hope we have in his faithfulness towards us.

Some may wonder why I mention truth and patience in the same breath. HOW does declaring truth over one's life prepare him/her to withstand temptations? Consider this: God is truth. (John 14:6; John 16:13; John 17:17) Sin is contrary to that of God's Spirit, therefore, all sin and the temptations of sin are based upon lies. When you give in to a temptation, for a short instant, you believe in a lie and apply it to your life. Jesus said in Matthew 12:34b, "For out of the abundance of the heart the mouth speaketh." The "heart" in scripture typically refers to "one's emotions," and most emotions are formed by one's beliefs. This topic will be covered more in depth in the Mindset Deliverance section at the end of the book. For now, my point in this is to say that what you choose to believe tends to always dictate your actions. If you continuously remember that you're saved, redeemed, justified, and empowered by Christ, you will not have fear nor deviate from Christ into sinful actions. It becomes easier to deal with temptations, even to the point where enough patience is developed that they will no longer be temptations!

# CHAPTER FIVE: CHOSEN

"God always moves first. He chooses us. We must BECOME HIS WILL and choose him as well, in relationship. Then God fulfills his promise to save us and restore us into our original nature, which is being called to be holy."

Romans 8:30: "Moreover whom he did predestinate, them he also called: and whom he called, them he also justified: and whom he justified, them he also glorified." This verse represents God's will within the four elements of time: before the concept of time was created (because God always knew everything before the concept of time, he predestined in his knowledge of whom he knew would choose him); the beginning of time, setting up the foundations of the earth and the motion of cause and effect which would lead to his plan of Christ's sacrifice for us (before any believer knows Christ, he/she is eventually called to be holy by accepting Christ); while we live in the present moment and receive justification by believing in Christ, daily conforming our minds to that belief in Christ; and the future hope and promise of glory when Christ returns to set up his kingdom upon the earth.

Some scientifically-minded people can think that the

argument of predestination absolves our personal responsibilities to the decisions that we make. What these individuals don't seem to understand is that because God made us in his image and likeness, like him, we have the power of choice, despite the fact that God predestined those of whom he knows will choose him. Then they'll argue that since God knows everything and affects the world with his knowledge of predestination, that eliminates the existence of our freedom of choice. The truth is that God, in his all-powerful sovereignty, is able to set everything in motion, makes promises of blessings and curses, knows what the choices are and how people will choose, and yet steps back to let us choose.

God rarely tells people their future choices outside of the purpose of glorifying his own name's sake. For instance, Matthew 26:34-35 shows the exchange between Jesus and Peter before Christ's crucifixion. "Jesus said unto him, Verily I say unto thee, That this night, before the cock crow, thou shalt deny me thrice. Peter said unto him, Though I should die with thee, yet will I not deny thee. Likewise also said all the disciples." If you don't know the story, Peter denies Christ three different times during the night when different people recognized him and asked, "Aren't you one of the disciples of Jesus?" My question about this is, "Would Peter have denied Jesus if he didn't tell Peter about his future?" Undoubtedly, yes. Peter would have made the same choices, not because he was predestined to make those choices, but because it was on Peter's heart to react that way to preserve his own life. Jesus simply knew it. The fact that Jesus told this to Peter was for his name's sake, to break Peter's old heart posture, and bring him into the heart posture to receive forgiveness and change into an unshakeable man of God after Jesus was resurrected. We see how unshakeable Peter is in Acts chapter 2 when he preaches the first sermon about Jesus, converting 3000 in attendance to repent and be baptized for the remissions of sins. Peter continued to remain unshakeable even unto his death.

I close this point with this: The apostles were told by Jesus to wait in Jerusalem in order to receive the baptism of the Holy Spirit and power. The reason they were chosen as the first to receive the baptism of the Holy Spirit is because they were the first ones who believed in Jesus and chose him. Nobody else would have received the Holy Spirit until the disciples preached Jesus to the masses. Jesus knew the disciples would choose him; he chose them first, and they chose him back. Being chosen is not a once-and-done deal. It is a daily action of continuously choosing Christ. This Word goes right into what God chooses us to become through Christ: called to be holy.

# CHAPTER SIX: CALLED TO BE HOLY

"Just like the Nazarene vow, our willingness to become holy to glorify God must be our nature. There is no temple (inside which to ritualistically sacrifice) where we can stop the vow we have with God, so our bodies and spirits are his temples forever, just as Christ is our high priest forever. Who would want the vow to stop anyway? Instead of hair and burnt offerings, we offer up everything we are, our identities, our purposes, our lives, dying with Christ and living because of him."

In Numbers chapter 6, God is describing more laws to Moses concerning Israel of which they are to keep. This chapter is special, though. It describes the Nazarene vow, one of the only laws you'll find that involves voluntary submission. The people literally didn't have to perform it, but to those who chose to perform it, they were taught how to do it right in order to glorify God in their submission. You will gain more insight if you read the whole chapter yourself, but I will do my best to paraphrase it for you. Basically, those who choose to perform the Nazarene vow must have absolutely no contact of eating or drinking anything from the vine: no grapes, no wine, no vinegar of wine, no strong drink, nothing from the vine tree or of the "kernels even to the husk." While performing this vow, a Nazarite was to not become unclean at all, either by touching or eating things that are unclean, including touching dead bodies. During this time, he/she was considered AS HOLY, following all the statutes laid upon him/her. He/she was not to shave any hair that grew on the head until the "time of separation" came to pass. This period of time leading up to the separation can be compared to cooking a stew in a crockpot. The longer you keep the stew cooking, the more tender the meat becomes, and the better the meal is. This was significant once the time of separation had passed, because the person performing the vow chose how long the time of separation of the vow was to take place, thereby varying the "tenderness" of the sacrifice. I'm using both meanings of that word for this analogy. How long a person abstained from uncleanliness was a testament to how much he/she cared about what was being offered to God through the sacrifices and the grown-out hair. The grown-out hair carried this holiness. At the end of the vow, multiple sacrifices and offerings would be made in the temple/tabernacle: the burnt offering; the sin offering; and the peace offering. The hair from the head would be shaved and thrown on top of the fire of the peace offering. This can relate to the fact that our desire to be holy is connected to the peace we attain from God through the sacrifice of Jesus Christ.

There are signs that Jesus performed the Nazarene vow as well. Close to his death, during the Passover feast, Mark 14:25 is a good hint that Jesus was accommodating his already holy existence with physical preparations of this vow. "Verily I say unto you, I will drink no more of the fruit of the vine, until that day that I drink it new in the kingdom of God." Jesus is the perfect example of what it means to be holy, yet it's probable in this logic that he still performed a vow of which in its very precepts declares a person AS HOLY before the sacrifice is provided. In this case, he was the sacrifice as well.

Romans 12:1-2 sheds light on the fact that our relationship with the Holy Spirit is comparative to that of living out the Nazarene vow forever. "I beseech you therefore, brethren, by the mercies of God, that ye present your bodies a living sacrifice, holy, acceptable unto God, which is your reasonable service. And be not conformed to this world: but be ye transformed by the renewing of your mind, that ye may prove what is that good, and acceptable, and perfect, will of God." We can reason these two verses backwards to get a full thought, comparing to the subject of the vow. The will of God is that we become transformed the by renewing of our minds so that we do not conform to the world; renewing our minds is possible because of his mercy (provided through the death and resurrection of Jesus Christ), and our bodies are able to become alive and holy, thereby being just like Christ, an acceptable sacrifice unto God when our bodies do physically die.

In those verses, when does it say we need to stop being transformed by the renewing of our minds? It doesn't! Not being conformed to the nature of the world is a continuous trait! A vow is not a once-and-done deal. It becomes who you are until you break it. This is what makes being a lukewarm Christian so dangerous because choosing to be conformed to the nature of the world up to the time of death proves that the lukewarm Christian is not an acceptable sacrifice to God when the body dies because he/she will not have wanted to be like Christ or overcome the world in order to fully believe in Christ. The later explanation of the Armor of God will expound upon this understanding.

# CHAPTER SEVEN: PROPHET

"Numbers 11:29 shows that those who carry God's Spirit should be prophets. What does it take to be a prophet? Humility is the first characteristic. Authority in one's function in God is the next. If God commands you to fulfill something, he is giving you authority and ability to do so! The humility is towards God; the authority is towards people. Purpose is the third. We aren't servants; we are friends. Yet we are humble enough to know that God has a specific plan for our lives to fulfill purposes."

In Numbers 11, the Israelites were complaining...again. Moses was fed up and asked God to give him relief. God told Moses in verse 17 to gather seventy trusted elders of the people, and he would take of the spirit that was on Moses and put it also on the elders as well to help him govern the people. In verse 25, the spirit rested upon the elders, and they did not stop prophesying. Two of the seventy who received the spirit were prophesying to people in the camp instead of the tabernacle. When Joshua told Moses about this, he told Moses to rebuke them. Moses replies in verse 29, "Enviest thou for my sake? would God that all the LORD's people were prophets, and that the LORD would put his spirit upon them!"

When I read this verse, I experienced a revelation about how much power God is willing to give his people. This verse coincides with 1 Corinthians chapter 12, talking about the gifts of the Spirit. Even though different people in the body of Christ attain particular offices of ministry (refer to Ephesians 4:11-16), it is the same Spirit of God who works all the gifts into every person (1 Corinthians 12:4-7), including the gift of prophecy. I deduce that this simple title of "prophet" in this verse as referred to the identity of the LORD's people is not speaking about an office of ministry, but of the structure of their character. I asked God, "What does it take to be a prophet?" When he led me to write the first short paragraph, the words simply flowed, and I wasn't sure where I'd find the necessary example to prove these characteristics. But I see now that Moses reveals these characteristics! "Enviest thou for my sake?" He was humble before God and made sure to give him the glory. He knew not to take credit for God's works, including what God did in Egypt to set Israel free. (This excludes when he frustratingly said to the people in Numbers 20:10, "Hear now, ye rebels; must we fetch you water out of this rock?" That very act of hitting the rock with his staff in order to make water flow from it the second time, disobeying God's command of speaking to the rock, and essentially taking credit for the miracle, is what kept Moses and Aaron from entering the promised land.)

Moses possessed both extremes of humility and lack thereof, so perhaps I should say that a SUCCESSFUL prophet has humility towards God. Moses carried out the authority given to him by God towards Pharoh and the Egyptians and then towards Israel up to the point of his death. This was all done through Moses for the purpose of glorifying God, a representation to the world that the God of Israel is the one true God. While these characteristics of humility, authority, and purpose could stand alone as Words of the Day, God made it a point to define "PROPHET" with these words. I also see that a characteristic of what a prophet has is the ability to hear God and then proclaim God's truth to others. This is one of the driving focuses of why God is having me write this book in the first place. I will explain "Rhema" and "Shama" later on in the Word of the Day, "REVELATION."

# CHAPTER EIGHT: JOY OF THE LORD

"The many verses about having joy during tribulations are not talking about some sick idea that we are supposed to love having a difficult life on earth. It's actually REDEFINING WHAT our lives are. Our identities are not our circumstances that we feel on earth or in our minds. Once we become saved by Christ, our joy is manifested in the fact that OUR IDENTITIES ARE NOW CHRIST. It doesn't matter if our bodies die while we're rich or poor, sick or healthy, loved or hated by people, still trying to get over addictions or not, etc. WE are alive in CHRIST, and that is our JOY!"

Joy seems to be highly underrated in this day and age. Often times, people focus on what makes them happy. Don't be confused, though. Happiness and joy are two different things. Joy creates happiness, but happiness does not always create joy. Happiness has everything to do with FEELINGS, and feelings are either chemically induced and/or are emotions that one chooses to have. Joy has everything to do with possessing LIFE PURPOSE. This makes sense logically, for the most part, but what does it say in the Bible about true joy and where it comes from?

Nehemiah 8:10: "Then he said unto them, Go your way,

eat the fat, and drink the sweet, and send portions unto them for whom nothing is prepared: for this day is holy unto our LORD: neither be ye sorry; for the joy of the LORD is your strength." If you decide not to read Nehemiah chapter 8, or even the book of Nehemiah at all, you can still gain some tingly feelings of assurance in the phrase, "for the joy of the LORD is your strength," but what does that even mean? We can see in Galatians 5:22-23 that joy is a fruit of God's Spirit. That, in turn, makes joy a descriptive characteristic of who God is. "But the fruit of the Spirit is love, joy, peace, longsuffering, gentleness, goodness, faith, meekness, temperance: against such there is no law." (Some of these fruits are Words of the Day as well; I will expound upon them further down the list. Just understand this point for future reference: anything that describes God's character is something that should define OUR identities as believers in Christ!)

It's very interesting that verse 23 ends with, "against such there is no law," because this actually ties into the context of Nehemiah chapter 8. Ezra and Nehemiah found themselves having an opportunity to teach the law of Moses to that particular generation of Israel because they had been scattered among nations and had never heard the law. Upon hearing it, Israel was sorrowful, which is what leads up to verse 10, basically sending a message saying, "Don't live in sorrow! Celebrate that God is willing to redeem you! Your strength is in God's joy, through which he is delighted to take back an obedient nation again!" That time period when the law was being taught describes the holy day (the feast lasts 8 days in total), the Feast of Tabernacles, and they learned how to abide by the customs set forth in the law. Nehemiah 8:17 sheds light on Israel's emotional state, saying, "And there was very great gladness," after having learned the laws and followed them in order to please God. "Against such there is no law," in Galatians 5:23 is basically saying that no Law comes against any of those fruits of the Spirit, inasmuch as we can also conclude that having these fruits of the Spirit fulfills the law because anything that does not break the law accomplishes the law. Concerning joy, this is my final point: the joy of the Lord inside us is a fruit of the Spirit that is made manifest by our desires of becoming RIGHTEOUS and living out righteousness in order to fulfill the life-purpose of pleasing God. What is righteousness, and what makes us righteous? Read on.

# CHAPTER NINE: RIGHTEOUS

"Do you believe in Christ and know him? Be assured that you are made righteous with Christ's righteousness. Condemnation, guilt, and shame do NOT belong to believers. When we feel condemnation, guilt, and shame, know this: God condemns the sin that's IN our FLESH. If you still operate your identity through your feelings and your flesh, you're going to feel what your flesh feels and think that condemnation is YOUR identity. This is why we must live IN the SPIRIT!"

The law of Moses has its place in the Judeo-Christian belief system. It has formed countries, shaped family lines, and sent evil societies to their complete and utter destruction. Jesus said in John 14:15, "If ye love me, keep my commandments." God used the law of Moses and the original 10 commandments to prove to himself who loved him or not, who chose to SEEK righteousness or iniquity. Paul says in Romans 4:2-3, "For if Abraham were justified by works, he hath whereof to glory; but not before God. For what saith the scripture? Abraham believed God, and it was counted unto him for righteousness." God counts the faith that it takes to follow his commandments as what makes one righteous, and this is true in the Old Covenant and New Covenant alike. Yet, carrying out the laws of Moses was simply meant to be a covering against God's wrath, not as a device to gain righteousness. Paul also says in Galatians 2:21, "I do not frustrate the grace of God: for if righteousness come by the law, then Christ is dead in vain." He continues his point about Abraham again in Galatians chapter 3, as well as reprimanding the Galatians for falling to the ideology that works is what justifies us into righteousness. Verses 6-7: "Even as Abraham believed God, and it was accounted to him for righteousness. Know ye therefore that they which are of faith, the same are the children of Abraham."

I really enjoy the conclusion in Galatians 3:21-29: "Is the law then against the promises of God? God forbid: for if there had been a law given which could have given life, verily righteousness should have been by the law. But the scripture hath concluded all under sin, that the promise by faith of Jesus Christ might be given to them that believe. But before faith came, we were kept under the law, shut up unto the faith which should afterwards be revealed. Wherefore the law was our schoolmaster to bring us unto Christ, that we might be justified by faith. But after that faith is come, we are no longer under a schoolmaster. For ye are all the children of God by faith in Christ Jesus. For as many of you as have been baptized into Christ have put on Christ. There is neither Jew nor Greek, there is neither bond nor free, there is neither male nor female: for ye are all one in Christ Jesus. And if ye be Christ's, then are ye Abraham's seed, and heirs according to the promise."

I am taking the time to write out all of these verses because without the correct understanding of what actually justifies us into righteousness, it will be very hard to apply the rest of the Words of the Day to our lives. This is because we can't (nor won't) do any works perfectly without Christ in us first. Christ is the only one in history who lived a completely sinless life and is the only one who went to heaven because of his good works. In Philippians chapter 3, Paul is using his own life as an example, concerning the fact that he had followed all the rules and was blameless concerning the law, but that he still missed the mark without having Christ. Philippians 3:7-12: "But what things were gain to me, those I counted loss for Christ. Yea doubtless, and I count all things but loss for the excellency of the knowledge of Christ Jesus my Lord: for whom I have suffered the loss of all things, and do count them but dung, that I may win Christ, and be found in him, not having mine own righteousness, which is of the law, but that which is through the faith of Christ, the righteousness which is of God by faith: that I may know him, and the power of his resurrection, and the fellowship of his sufferings, being made conformable unto his death; if by any means I might attain unto the resurrection of the dead. Not as though I had already attained, either were already perfect: but I follow after, if that I may apprehend that for which also I am apprehended of Christ Jesus." Righteousness is found in having faith in Christ, but I may also suggest that righteousness is found in having the actual faith OF Christ inside us as well. The distinction is made in verse 9 when he says, "That I may win Christ, and be found in him, not having MINE OWN RIGHTEOUSNESS, which is of the law, but that [righteousness] which is through the faith OF Christ..." If "faith of Christ" is supposed to mean that Paul is "having faith IN Christ," why would Paul highlight his lack of righteousness compared to the righteousness of Christ?

How do we attain the righteousness of Christ? Romans 10:9-12 says it plainly: "That if thou shalt confess with thy mouth the Lord Jesus, and shalt believe in thine heart that

God hath raised him from the dead, thou shalt be saved. For with the heart man believeth unto righteousness; and with the mouth confession is made unto salvation. For the scripture saith, Whosoever believeth on him shall not be ashamed. For there is no difference between the Jew and the Greek: for the same Lord over all is rich unto all that call upon him." When we attain this righteousness from Christ, what happens afterwards? Jeremiah 31:33: "But this shall be the covenant that I will make with the house of Israel; After those days, saith the LORD, I will put my law in their inward parts, and write it in their hearts; and will be their God, and they shall be my people." This Old Testament statement is clearly defining what will happen after Christ comes into the picture. Paul mirrored this in Hebrews 10:16-17: "This is the covenant that I will make with them after those days, saith the Lord, I will put my laws into their hearts, and in their minds will I write them; and their sins and iniquities will I remember no more." No sins or iniquities sounds like righteousness to me!

If Paul says that there is no righteousness attained directly from the law, what is it that enters us that can be considered untouchable by the law? Obviously, it is the Holy Spirit himself! John 14:15-17: "If ye love me, keep my commandments. And I will pray the Father, and he shall give you another Comforter, that he may abide with you for ever; even the Spirit of truth; whom the world cannot receive, because it seeth him not, neither knoweth him: but ye know him; for he dwelleth with you, and shall be in you." John 14:23+26: "If a man love me, he will keep my words: and my Father will love him, and we will come unto him, and make our abode with him... But the Comforter, which is the Holy Ghost, whom the Father will send in my name, he shall teach you all things, and bring all things to your remembrance, whatsoever I have said unto you." The law that is written on our hearts is Spirit and Truth, the complete Spirit of God inside us, where the fruits of the Spirit that are mentioned in Galatians 5:22-23 are to become our identities after believing in Christ and receiving God's Spirit. Those fruits of the Spirit are our laws!

Does Christ's interference in the process of the law that sentences people to eternal, spiritual death mean that the Law of Moses and the Ten Commandments are completely erased from existence? There are those who believe that because Christ came to "fulfill the law," that the Old Testament laws are completely erased. There are others who believe that Christ was only sent to fulfill the law and NOT abolish it, and thereby they think that we still have to follow the Old Testament laws with the help of the Holy Spirit inside of us. I'm going to suggest right now that it's somewhere in between and that the Old Covenant and the New Covenant exist AT THE SAME TIME! (Pretty bold claim! Read on to understand more!)

Follow this line of reasoning: If the Law of Moses and the Ten Commandments do not exist anymore, then what will God use to judge all people "according to their deeds" when all people will be in front of God in the last days, giving an account of their lives to him? (Revelation 20:12-15: "And I saw the dead, small and great, stand before God; and the books were opened: and another book was opened, which is the book of life: and the dead were judged out of those things which were written in the books, according to their works. And the sea gave up the dead which were in it; and death and hell delivered up the dead which were in them: and they were judged every man according to their works. And death and hell were cast into the lake of fire. This is the second death. And whosoever was not found written in the book of life was cast into the lake of fire.") Those who do not believe on Christ will be judged for their actions, so we can inversely decipher that those who do believe on Christ will not be judged for their works; they will be judged upon whether they have Christ's Spirit and then will be "passed over" like the Israelites in Egypt. (John 12:48: "He that rejecteth me, and receiveth not my words, hath one that judgeth him: the word that I have spoken, the same shall judge him in the last day.") Christ didn't come to abolish the law, but to fulfill the law so that he could usher in the New Covenant. (Matthew 5:17: "Think not that I am come to destroy the law, or the prophets: I am not come to destroy, but to fulfil.") Christ makes those who believe in him dead to the law. (Romans 7:4: "Wherefore, my brethren, ye also are become dead to the law by the body of Christ; that ye should be married to another, even to him who is raised from the dead, that we should bring forth fruit unto God.") We can understand that the law is not abolished for those who do not believe in him. (Romans 10:4: "For Christ is the end of the law for righteousness to every one that believeth.") If they do not believe in Christ, they are condemned already. (John 3:18: "He that believeth on him is not condemned: but he that believeth not is condemned already, because he hath not believed in the name of the only begotten Son of God.") They are condemned because those who operate under the law are required to follow the whole law. (Galatians 5:3: "For I testify again to every man that is circumcised, that he is a debtor to do the whole law.)

There are 613 laws depicted in the Old Testament, many of which are food laws and cleanliness laws (which are not bad to follow if applicable), but others are sacrificial laws that require us to know a Levite priest to which to give our animal sacrifices and represent us inside a tabernacle where the priest would burn the sacrifices for us. We'd all need a Levite and a tabernacle, and God knew that this would be impossible once he opened up salvation to be available to non-Jewish people. (This is why the royal priesthood is assigned to Jesus, and Jesus represents us in front of the Father.) I'm sure there are other laws that are not applicable to our modern society and people. The point I'm trying to make here is that if the capability of performing even one of the 613 laws of the Old Testament is non-existent, then it is impossible to keep the law as a whole. If it is impossible to keep the whole Torah (the law of Moses), then our fulfillment of the Torah through our own capabilities is not THE requirement for righteousness and continuously pleasing God. Let's consider the beginning of Galatians chapter 5 again for better understanding. Paul mentioned the law of circumcision because there were Messianic Jews who were preaching that the Greeks had to become Jewish first before receiving Christ. This tradition became a fallacy in this instance and was corrected. Although I'm sure that this didn't stop the tradition of circumcision in general among the Jews or even in general Christian practice, the fact that Paul did not mention WHEN the Greek believers SHOULD get circumcised must mean that circumcision can be seen as nothing more than a tradition when compared to keeping the "law of Christ."

1 John 3:23: "And this is his commandment, That we should believe on the name of his Son Jesus Christ, and love one another, as he gave us commandment." Continuing with the first line of reasoning as we look at 1 John 3:23, if keeping the commandment of believing in Christ grants us the ability of living in the Spirit and the Spirit living in us (1 John 2:27) and cancels our hellish judgement now that we are believers, then to live controlled by the flesh will lead to judgement of death WITH the law as the tool OF judgement. (Romans 8:6:

"For to be carnally minded is death; but to be spiritually minded is life and peace.") John 5:26-27: "For as the Father hath life in himself; so hath he given to the Son to have life in himself; and hath given him authority to execute judgement also, because he is the Son of man." "Because he is the Son of man," implies that Jesus has authority to judge the world in the end not only because he's God but because he was the only man to have fulfilled the law. He is worthy and acceptable on both accounts. So then, the Law THROUGH JESUS is the measuring stick by which all people will be judged. All will be assessed whether they have Christ, and if they do not have Christ, EVERY evil deed will be weighed against the Law, the Torah.

This leads me to my final point about righteousness. In order to live righteously, we must believe in Christ and then live BY the Spirit and not controlled by the flesh in order to produce in us the fruits of God's Spirit. Romans chapters 7 and 8 describe this very well; I suggest reading these chapters in depth to gain more understanding. For now, I'd like to highlight verses in Romans chapter 8. Verse 1: "There is therefore now no condemnation to them which are in Christ Jesus, who walk not after the flesh, but after the Spirit." "Walk not after the flesh, but after the Spirit," is describing what it is to be "in Christ Jesus." Verse 2: "For the law of the Spirit of life in Christ Jesus hath made me free from the law of sin and death." There are clearly two different laws highlighted here: the law of sin and death is the law of works, by which we cannot be justified; the "law of the Spirit of life in Christ Jesus" is the sacrifice of our flesh and desires BY believing in Christ and taking on the characteristics of his identity. (In fact, when we search the phrase "law of Christ" in the Bible, the one and only verse that contains this exact wording in the KJV is Galatians 6:2: "Bear ye one another's burdens, and so fulfil the law of Christ." In order to bear one another's burdens, it takes perfect love which can only be found in becoming God's Spiritual character.) Romans 8:3-4: "For what the law could not do, in that it was weak through the flesh, God sending his own Son in the likeness of sinful flesh, and for sin, condemned sin in the flesh: that the righteousness of the law might be fulfilled in us, who walk not after the flesh, but after the Spirit." God condemned sin "IN THE FLESH!" This is what I was referring in my original quote in the first paragraph. Imagine that sin is a person in jail, waiting for death row. The flesh is sin's cage. When the cage is destroyed as a sacrifice, sin is erased. Those who remained righteous by believing in Christ and living in the Spirit will receive their bodies back (or new bodies) in heaven, glorified without sin trapped inside. (In fact, if it can be understood that the only way to ATTAIN righteousness is through believing in Jesus Christ, then it can be understood that the only way to RETAIN righteousness is by continuing to believe in Jesus Christ. The same simple Gospel that saves us is the only thing that can maintain us! I will cover more of this topic of "retaining salvation" in the ARMOR OF GOD section.) Those who lived cold or lukewarm lives, who walked out their lives being controlled by the flesh, they are in danger of being erased WITH the sin that is in the flesh because they will have adhered themselves (their spirits) to the flesh. (See Romans 11:20-23 to understand how God grafts those who are faithful into "the tree" and those who don't live in faith are able to be cut off.)

Romans 8:4 explains a really important point about sin being "condemned in the flesh." Although the transliteration of "condemned sin in the flesh" should be understood as something like "condemned sin that happens to be in the flesh," I believe it's important to understand that sin is condemned TO the flesh as well because the sin in the flesh does not leave the body. If that sin in the flesh were able to leave, Christians would never be able to die of things like old age, for example. This is because sin leads to death. So, the fact that all Christians since the early church era have died basically proves that sin is caged to the body. This sin is ready to kill the flesh similarly to how Jesus had let the Jews kill him. Romans 8:10: "And if Christ be in you, the body is dead because of sin; but the Spirit is life because of righteousness." This has everything to do with the Nazarene vow! In fact, I was tempted to explain Romans 8:4 in that section, but it wouldn't have made sense without explaining righteousness first. The reason why sin is condemned to the flesh is to fulfill our part in our Nazarene vow, in that the righteousness that DOES exist in the purpose of the Old Covenant law would be fulfilled when we live our lives in the identity of Christ's Spirit. The exaction of the fruit of the Spirit in our lives is just like the sacrifice of one's hair offered as a peace offering during the Nazarene vow.

To explain it a little better, because Christ fulfilled the law in his death and resurrection, when we believe in Christ, we are fulfilling the Old Covenant laws as a whole when we live out the fruits of the Spirit through Christ's Spirit. This includes laws like the cleanliness laws, sacrificial laws, the Sabbath, etc. James 2:18 says, "Yea, a man may say, Thou has faith, and I have works: shew me thy faith without thy works, and I will shew thee my faith by my works." The "works" that this verse and most of the book of James is talking about is the result of believing in Christ and living in the Spirit, performing works that emulate the fruit of God's Spirit. This fruit fulfills the purpose of the Old Covenant laws of loving God with all our hearts and loving our neighbors.

In conclusion, I'm reminded of a story Todd White told during a sermon. [2] He was apologizing for not preaching a vital point concerning the gospel of Christ. It was a life-changing event to realize this error. As he was being corrected in his spirit, he said to God, "This really hurts!" God said to him, "It wouldn't hurt if you were dead." I believe what God was saying to him was that of being dead to the flesh. Most of Romans chapter 6 refers to "dying to the flesh so that we may live through Jesus." Romans 6:11-12: "Likewise reckon ye also yourselves to be dead indeed unto sin, but alive unto God through Jesus Christ our Lord. Let not sin therefore reign in your mortal body, that ye should obey it in the lusts thereof." Thank God that the law of sin and death does not reign over believers! Galatians 5:5-6: "For we through the Spirit wait for the hope of righteousness by faith. For in Jesus Christ neither circumcision availeth any thing, nor uncircumcision; but faith which worketh by love."

If you live controlled by the flesh, you will feel and go through the judgements that are laid upon the flesh. You will live without feeling condemnation if you live by faith in the Spirit.

# CHAPTER TEN: HONESTY

"Refer to 1 John 4:17-20. This reference can't exist in us without attaining honesty towards our growth and towards others concerning the TRUTH of the GOSPEL that is in Jesus. And because of Jesus, we have perfect love while operating in him. 1 Corinthians 13:6 also says that love doesn't have joy in evil but delights in the truth."

1 John 4:17-21: "Herein is our love made perfect, that we may have boldness in the day of judgement: because as he is, so are we in this world. There is no fear in love; but perfect love casteth out fear: because fear hath torment. He that feareth is not made perfect in love. We love him, because he first loved us. If a man say, I love God, and hateth his brother, he is a liar: for he that loveth not his brother whom he hath seen, how can he love God whom he hath not seen? And this commandment have we from him, That he who loveth God love his brother also."

1 Corinthians 13:6: "Charity [Love] rejoiceth not in iniquity, but rejoiceth in the truth;"

The reason why truth and love are used in the same context in 1 John 4:17-20 is because love cannot function in lies. God is the Spirit of Truth. In him is no lie; all things that are contrary to him are based in lies. True love is found in the gospel of Christ, in that, "Greater love hath no man than this, that a man lay down his life for his friends." -John 15:12. Jesus is the ultimate example of love where the Father sent his Son to die for all mankind. Love is pointless without being shared with others. Since we are commanded to love God by loving people, our identities must be crystal clear and honest so that we glorify the truth of the gospel as we share that truth and love with others through our words and actions.

# CHAPTER ELEVEN: AMENDS

"We are made new. All the old things pass away after accepting Christ, but sometimes faults of the past still live inside other people's hearts. When we are reconciled in Christ, he prepares the ways and opportunities for us to reconcile with people in our pasts. Just like the idea that we love other people because we love God, so will it become a desire for us to reconcile unto other people in our pasts just as we reconcile ourselves with God."

2 Corinthians 5:17-21: "Therefore if any man be in Christ, he is a new creature: old things are passed away; behold, all things are become new. And all things are of God, who hath reconciled us to himself by Jesus Christ, and hath given to us the ministry of reconciliation; to wit, that God was in Christ, reconciling the world unto himself, not imputing their trespasses unto them; and hath committed unto us the word of reconciliation. Now then we are ambassadors for Christ, as though God did beseech you by us: we pray you in Christ's stead, be ye reconciled to God. For he hath made him to be sin for us, who knew no sin; that we might be made the righteousness of God in him."

"Reconciliation" is the act of reestablishing a close

relationship between two people or to settle a debt. In this case between us and God, both definitions apply. God "reconciled us to himself by Jesus Christ" in that our relationship with God is mended when Christ's sacrifice and resurrection makes believers "the righteousness of God." So, the act of making amends has everything to do with forgiveness between two people, forgiving the debts, forgiving the hard feelings, etc.

The perfect story behind this thought is the parable of the unforgiving servant in Matthew 18:21-35. "Then came Peter to him, and said, Lord, how oft shall my brother sin against me, and I forgive him? till seven times? Jesus saith unto him, I say not unto thee, Until seven times: but, until seventy times seven." ("Seventy times seven" is considered as an expression in this context that means to never stop forgiving.) "Therefore is the kingdom of heaven likened unto a certain king, which would take account of his servants. And when he had begun to reckon, one was brought unto him, which owed him ten thousand talents." (Ten thousand talents of currency compared to today's modern currency could be millions if not billions of dollars!) "But forasmuch as he had not to pay, his lord commanded him to be sold, and his wife, and children, and all that he had, and payment to be made. The servant therefore fell down, and worshipped him, saying, Lord, have patience with me, and I will pay thee all. Then the lord of that servant was moved with compassion, and loosed him, and forgave him the debt. But the same servant went out, and found one of his fellowservants, which owed him an hundred pence: and he laid hands on him, and took him by the throat, saying, Pay me that thou owest. And his fellowservant fell down at his feet, and besought him, saying, Have patience with me, and I will pay thee all. And he would not: but went and cast him into prison, till he should pay the debt. So when his fellowservants saw what was done, they were very sorry, and came and told unto their lord all that was done. Then his lord, after that he had called him, said unto him, O thou wicked servant, I forgave thee all that debt, because thou desiredst me: shouldest not thou also have had compassion on thy fellowservant, even as I had pity on thee? And his lord was wroth, and delivered him to the tormentors, till he should pay all that was due unto him. So likewise shall my heavenly Father do also unto you, if ye from your hearts forgive not every one his brother their trespasses."

What are the feelings and characteristics behind unrighteous unforgiveness? (Only God can retain unforgiveness righteously without giving into sinful emotions because he is the only one to which all people owe a life-debt...and he is without sin.) Anger, hate, pride, contempt, self-righteousness, condemnation? I'm sure there's more to unforgiveness than meets the eye, but one thing that is clear is that having an unforgiving heart is contrary to that of the heart of God. Even though God has every right to not forgive humanity for its life-debt, he still supplied every means possible for us to receive forgiveness through Christ. When we receive the Holy Spirit by believing in Christ, he has reconciled us unto himself. He will then search our hearts for any sin that exists in it and expel it from his presence. The Holy Spirit teaches us all things and reveals all things as is needed in our lives. (John 14:26) So, when we are living completely by the Spirit, we will hear his groanings in our hearts; if there is unforgiveness, he will show us with whom to make amends.

"So likewise shall my heavenly Father do also unto you, if ye from your hearts forgive not every one his brother their trespasses." This last sentence of the story reveals an important point. Sometimes it is impossible to reach out to certain people to whom we need to extend forgiveness in real life. Sometimes they're dead. Sometimes they have blocked us completely out of their lives. Sometimes it would be completely dangerous to go up to someone and forgive them when they did not ask for forgiveness (they will not take you seriously and purposely continue to do the very thing that hurts you, such as cheating on you in a relationship, which could have terrible consequences if you share children with them). Sometimes they don't believe that they did anything wrong and refuse to make amends if others still believe in their guilt. Before, during, and after any of these kinds of situations, forgiving those people in our hearts is the most important thing to keep us right with God in our relationship with him. If we refuse to forgive others in our hearts after we discover our unforgiveness, we're missing the mark of being God's love towards others. They don't even have to know that we've forgiven them in our hearts! Though, God will provide the opportunities for us to extend forgiveness to others if possible; sometimes the one thing that releases those people from their own unforgiveness is knowing that they are forgiven. Even if making amends does not restore one's relationship with the other, it's totally within God's love for both parties that their hearts are made right in forgiveness. Ask God what is supposed to be restored or left alone. Each situation is totally different and needs to be led by the Holy Spirit.

# CHAPTER TWELVE: CARNALITY

"This is a warning, the first in this list. It could have been stated with the word "spirit," as in, live by the Spirit and not the flesh, but God wants to highlight this word "carnality" as "spiritual cancer." Carnality leads to death. In attempts to save your body, you will likely lose your soul and/or what it takes to have faith in Christ. You can't trust God if you have a double mind, which is like having thoughts of spiritual goals that are led by physical desires and outcomes."

In Matthew 16:21-27, Jesus tells the disciples God's plan that Jesus would be killed and raised on the third day. Peter speaks out in a very carnal mindset, in that he refused to accept that this should happen to Jesus. One could assume that Peter was speaking out against this foretelling because he was afraid of losing Jesus or wanted to protect him. Verse 23: "But he turned, and said unto Peter, Get thee behind me, Satan: thou art an offence unto me: for thou savourest not the things that be of God, but those that be of men." The literal meaning of "Satan" is "one who is opposed." He was saying that Peter's mindset was completely contrary to the will of God. Desiring to please the flesh and adhering to one's feelings in this case is a clear depiction of what "carnality" means, and Jesus clarifies further in the next verses. Verses 24-27: "Then said Jesus unto his disciples, If any man will come after me, let him deny himself, and take up his cross, and follow me. For whosoever will save his life shall lose it: and whosoever will lose his life for my sake shall find it. For what is a man profited, if he shall gain the whole world, and lose his own soul? or what shall a man give in exchange for his soul? For the Son of man shall come in the glory of his Father with his angels; and then he shall reward every man according to his works."

As I've already covered in the Word of the Day "RIGHTEOUS," the "works" that believers will be judged by is not "our" works, but we will be reviewed to see if we believe in Christ, the one who did all the righteous works. James 4:7-8 gives us an idea of what it's like to not be carnal when we consider our belief in Christ. "Submit yourselves therefore to God. Resist the devil, and he will flee from you. Draw nigh to God, and he will draw nigh to you. Cleanse your hands, ye sinners; and purify your hearts, ye double minded." "Sinners" are obviously those who do not believe in Christ; James tells them to cleanse their hands, presumably with belief in the works of Christ's hands. "Double minded" people are those who have belief in Christ but try to serve two masters: lukewarm or hypocritical Christians. (Matthew 6:24: "No man can serve two masters: for either he will hate the one, and love the other; or else he will hold to the one, and despise the other. Ye cannot serve God and mammon." 1 Corinthians 10:21: "Ye cannot drink the cup of the Lord, and the cup of devils: ye cannot be partakers of the Lord's table, and of the table of devils.") James' instruction to them is to purify their hearts. The "heart" most commonly refers to one's mind and emotions, one's thoughts and feelings about what he/she believes is true. So, when James says, "Purify your hearts," he is saying that double-minded people should shift their mindsets and beliefs onto that which is completely true. Complete truth is found through Jesus Christ and every word that comes from the Father. Adhering to everything that is true in Christ is how we resist carnality and expel sinful mindsets!

# CHAPTER THIRTEEN: MOURN

"There aren't many verses that say that God mourns, but there are verses that talk about how God cares about even our smallest problems and needs. He's telling me directly that he does mourn for those who don't choose him, but his justice prevails. Having his heart means that we feel this mourning sometimes. Live in his joy; use his mourning as inspiration to reach those who haven't chosen him."

Matthew 6:25-26: "Therefore I say unto you, Take no thought for your life, what ye shall eat, or what ye shall drink; nor yet for your body, what ye shall put on. Is not the life more than meat, and the body than raiment? Behold the fowls of the air: for they sow not, neither do they reap, nor gather into barns; yet your heavenly Father feedeth them. Are ye not much better than they?"

God's love is pure. John 3:16 says, "For God so loved the world, that he gave his only begotten Son, that whosoever believeth in him should not perish, but have everlasting life." God knows that not all people will choose Christ in order to be saved, but he made Christ available to all people anyway. Luke 15:7: "I say unto you, that likewise joy shall be in heaven over one sinner that repenteth, more than over ninety and nine just persons, which need no repentance." I believe that if God can feel righteous joy for a new believer, he can feel righteous mourning for those who are lost to sin and death. I highlight the word "righteous" because some people mourn out of fear and other negative emotions. There is no such emotion in God's character. His mourning is generated from his love. God's love is inside us; allow yourself to be led by his love to reach those for which he mourns.

# CHAPTER FOURTEEN: FREEDOM

"Our chains are cut from bondage when we believe in Christ, but sometimes we hold onto the chains. We experience true freedom when we let go of everything from the past in the forgiveness we have from the FATHER. Our wills are not our own; they are a copy of his will. Having freedom in deliverance creates opportunities to grow BOLDNESS."

John 8:31-32: "Then said Jesus to those Jews which believed on him, If ye continue in my word, then are ye my disciples indeed; and ye shall know the truth, and the truth shall make you free." Jesus was preaching to a multitude of Jews and said the above statements to them. The rest of the dialogue gets pretty dicey and sarcastic when some of the Jews take offense to his words, as they assumed that they already knew the truth. Putting that aside, Jesus states something pivotal concerning the nature of freedom that believers can have. The stipulation behind attaining true freedom in this context is "if ye continue in my word." God's words are truth; Jesus spoke nothing but what the Father told him to say. So, when we continue in his word, we are adhering to the truth, which is what Jesus said right after, in that "ye shall know the truth, and the truth shall make you free." Choosing Jesus—choosing truth—is not something that we simply do once, although there has to be an initial moment in time when we begin to choose. It is something that we do continuously every day, forever.

One step further, Jesus said in John 17:3, "And this is life eternal, that they might know thee the only true God, and Jesus Christ, whom thou hast sent." I'll be repeating this verse in a lot of topics because it is that good! Concerning John 8:31-32, when he says that if we continue in his words and know truth, that can literally mean that if we adhere to his every word, we will KNOW God!

I used to be interested in astrology when I was younger. I found it very interesting that the characteristics of all of my 20+ signs were very accurate in describing my actual personality. Witchcrafts and other forms of manipulation of power exist; there are too many examples in the Bible showcasing how the devil interacts with the world. But these interactions are obviously contrary to God and are based in lies. In the past two years, my relationship with God had grown exponentially, and I started to disconnect from things that were based in lies and sin. I found out that the stronger my relationship with God had become, the less I identified with my astrological signs! The costs of witchcraft (and the like) are high, usually consisting of selling one's soul, trading fortunes, making deals, someone dying, etc. It is a very caging existence. The more that we live in the Spirit, the more that truth becomes a part of our Christian identities, and the freer we become! Of course, believing in Christ makes us free as new creatures, but our free will must come into alignment with God's will in the process of renewing our minds in order to attain growing freedoms while we represent his kingdom on earth! (For example, a sex addict who becomes a Christian will still have to learn how to progressively surrender his/her habits in order to attain more freedom from the addiction, until it is finally gone.)

Living in freedom has EVERYTHING to do with renewing the mind. Consider renewal of the mind as if like a blood transfusion. In a blood transfusion, infected blood is syphoned out while healthy blood is injected. When the mind is renewed, one believes truth while disbelieving and renouncing the lies that had been previously accepted. In this, we fulfil the charge in 2 Corinthians 10:5 that says, bring "into captivity every thought to the obedience of Christ." Christ is our "truth filter," and demonic influences that are invited by the lies to which we previously adhered have no ground on which to stand and have to flee at the mention of Jesus' name!

# CHAPTER FIFTEEN: BOLDNESS

"In boldness, there is purpose, power, and passion through the moving of the Holy Spirit in us towards others. We are not afraid of the Gospel! It is truth, our identity. We are not afraid of other people's opinions. We approach their opinions with love and slap those opinions in the face with God's shield of faith in an experience that God gives to them. Our boldness is simply our confidence in his truth, confidence in what he desires for us to perform and to be, not a reason to rush in without consulting God. Boldly consult God. Boldly carry out what he says. True love casts out ALL fear; God is love; boldly we are his love towards others."

As I've been writing this book, God has been teaching me over and over again that all of these Words of the Day have very little to do with who we are initially and have EVERYTHING to do with who CHRIST is! Christ is fearless in his purpose. Although he experienced human fear when he was praying in the Garden of Gethsemane before his time on the cross approached, he quickly stuck with his purpose and prayed, "Nevertheless not as I will, but as thou wilt." (Matthew 26:39)

Just like Paul said in Romans 1:16, we should "not be

ashamed of the gospel of Christ: for it is the power of God unto salvation to every one that believeth;" In this, among other verses, we understand where our boldness is directed: the purpose of spreading the truth about Christ's death, resurrection, and salvation through him. Matthew 28:18-20: "And Jesus came and spake unto them, saying, All power is given unto me in heaven and in earth. Go ye therefore, and teach all nations, baptizing them in the name of the Father, and of the Son, and of the Holy Ghost: teaching them to observe all things whatsoever I have commanded you: and, lo, I am with you always, even unto the end of the world." Jesus also said in John 14:12-14, "Verily, verily, I say unto you, He that believeth on me, the works that I do shall he do also; and greater works than these shall he do; because I go unto my Father. And whatsoever ye shall ask in my name, that will I do, that the Father may be glorified in the Son. If ye shall ask any thing in my name, I will do it." These verses in John highlight the Great Commission Jesus gave in Matthew in relation to when he said, "because I go unto my Father." When he spoke to the disciples before his ascension, it's significant that Jesus declared, "All power is given unto me in heaven and in earth."

Why would Jesus declare his own power first before instructing the disciples (and subsequently all future believers) to go into all the world to make disciples in every nation? As I've mentioned before, when God gives a command or instruction, he is giving us power and authority to do as he spoke. I believe that the power and authority as it comes to performing miracles and spreading the truth of the gospel is FROM Jesus in the Holy Spirit inside us, doing all things THROUGH us of which we ask of him. Just as Christ was fearless on earth to live out the purpose that God had given him, so we should be fearless in boldly pronouncing our faith and testimonies in the truth of Christ, unashamed of what people might think about us...because WE are not the ones who are reaching them. Christ reaches them through us. Boldly ask him to fulfill his promises so that his love for all will give people faith to carry his flame! He will teach us what to do and speak.

Philippians 4:13: "I can do all things through Christ which strengtheneth me."

# CHAPTER SIXTEEN: AFFIRMATION

"Sometimes we decide that our lives are better with words of affirmation from other people, but is it always the truth? The only words that should matter are God's words; they are truth. Since there is power in words, and since we are in relationship with God, our words carry the same power in truth. Just like God wants us to be bold in the truth of the Gospel, he wants us to be bold in AFFIRMING his truths out loud to ourselves."

Proverbs 18:21: "Death and life are in the power of the tongue: and they that love it shall eat the fruit thereof."

Psalm 118:8: "It is better to trust in the LORD than to put confidence in man."

John 6:63b: "the words that I speak unto you, they are spirit, and they are life."

John 14:10: "Believest thou not that I am in the Father, and the Father in me? the words that I speak unto you I speak not of myself: but the Father that dwelleth in me, he doeth the works."

Considering the above verses, I would deduce that if the words that Jesus spoke were spirit and life because they were truths that came from the Father, then words that are rooted from the confidence in the corruptible, fleshly man are words of death. There is nothing of which we could believe and say that would lead to life without God's truth intervening in us.

I will never question the order in which the Holy Spirit leads. I had a feeling that I would receive forty Words of the Day by the end of the Fast, but I couldn't be too sure. As I got into a flow of listening to him speak to me in various ways and knowing when to write certain words down, he gave me "AFFIRMATION" so much later than I would have imagined, but it was exactly what I needed during my lessons about deliverance. God was stripping me of lies that had been implanted into my beliefs, but God could only go so far without impeding upon my free will. So, he had to teach me how to denounce the lies. Personally, I was very critical of myself and my abilities. Although I had learned a year and a half before that I was not worthy of condemnation anymore because I believe in Christ, that didn't stop me from setting the bar too high for myself. I believed many things that were true in the Bible, but I had neglected to speak truth over my life so that I could be totally free from the lies! This was also a time when I had learned that I suffered from a habit of being codependent of people. I thought that my worth was based in the fact that God loves me, but I ACTED like my worth was based in what other people thought about me.

If it isn't already clear enough, the words that we speak are important in maintaining and building our lives here on this earth and in our spiritual home. This understanding can be related to what secularism calls "The Law of Attraction." I am willing to bet that whomever came up with the idea of this "law" stole it from Proverbs 18:21! This "law" is all about picking a reality you want to have and then speaking things into the reality of your existence, much like living by the motto of, "If you don't ask, you won't receive." But what GOOD will come from a fleshly, sinful man's words if speaking is used to create his reality? What good will come of a drug addict who speaks a winning lottery ticket into his life when he clearly needs to be delivered from a horrible addiction first?! We should NEVER speak a new reality into our lives using this weird religion of the law of attraction (although I believe that Christians do this in general while operating from God's heart and declaring the name of Jesus). We need to wholeheartedly seek God's truth to transform us from the inside out, delivering us from the evil which was left over from our past lives that ensnares our minds in the form of habits. Deliverance NEEDS TO BE ROOTED in the TRUTHS OF GOD! If ANYTHING is rooted in death, it did not come from God, but it WAS PURCHASED with the blood of Christ! It needs to be surrendered to him.

Located near the end of this book, I have written what I call the "COMPLETE AFFIRMATIONS LIST." The whole list is based off of Bible verses that help you declare your identity to yourself and to God. My plan for myself was to speak this affirmations list over my life until I finally started living out my identity in Christ. Now I plan on just rereading this whole book whenever I need to be reminded of my identity if I were to ever fall off track. I'd suggest that you do the same!

# CHAPTER SEVENTEEN: LISTENING

"John 17:3 says that knowing the Holy Spirit is eternal life. What does it take to know him? If we can't see God, all we have is the faith we get by the experiences that he gives us. If that's the case, then the only way we can know him is by consistently listening and learning what his voice sounds like through constant communion. We know what his voice SHOULD sound like because he tells us who he is in the Bible. Avoid all distractions and cling onto what you know is truly God's voice."

Listening to God is an integral part of the Christian walk. In my studies, I couldn't find a single source undeniably proving that God never stops talking to us or that he would decide to remain silent at any given point. What governs our knowledge of such things? Even when I researched the famous "400 years of silence" topic (when God was supposedly silent between the time period of Malachi and John the Baptist), in my opinion, it seems that the only thing that dictated if God was actually silent with Israel was Israel's ability to hear God or not. Of course, God can do whatever he wants! With this Word of the Day, I will list all the different ways that God talks; we will also discuss the different reasons why God would choose to remain silent. This section is all about what we need in order to hear God. The Word of the Day, "REVELATION," will be about our purpose in what we DO with what we hear from God.

So, how does God speak?

## AUDIBLY

He is very capable of speaking audibly to people, however soft or loud. Exodus 19:9+16: "And the LORD said unto Moses, Lo, I come unto thee in a thick cloud, that the people may hear when I speak with thee, and believe thee for ever. And Moses told the words of the people unto the LORD... And it came to pass on the third day in the morning, that there were thunders and lightnings, and a thick cloud upon the mount, and the voice of the trumpet exceeding loud; so that all people that was in the camp trembled." The Lord also whispered to Elijah in the mountain caves where he was hiding. (1 Kings 19:11-13)

For the sake of answering the critics' question, "Does God speak audibly now in modern times?" I would argue that anything that was done after the death and resurrection of Christ, during the beginnings of the early church, is allowed to be done in our modern day, too. There is nothing that limits God in prophecy or promise. So, a good example where God had spoken audibly in the New Testament is when Jesus knocked Saul off his horse in Act 9:3-7. The two men who were traveling with Saul were speechless because they heard the voice of the Lord as well, but I believe it is unclear if they saw the light as well, based on the wording of scripture, and also the fact that Saul was the only one who was knocked down and blinded.

## FEELINGS

God can speak to us in multiple ways through our

physical feelings. Acts 17:27: "That they should seek the Lord, if haply they might feel after him, and find him, though he be not far from every one of us:" This verse leaves room for opportunity of different types of feelings to be affected; those who seek the Lord might find him by following feelings that are given to them. Knowing the Lord's voice is VERY IMPORTANT in this instance because the devil is keen on twisting God's words by speaking like God but then spewing half-truths to us. When it comes to hearing information from outside sources, if the information received is not evident of God's character, then it is not from God. John 10:14: "I am the good shepherd, and know my sheep, and am known of mine." When we hear the Lord, we will KNOW it is him! God is not a God of doubt; he is a God of CERTAINTY. Daniel 2:22: "He revealeth the deep and secret things: he knoweth what is in the darkness, and the light dwelleth with him." God is certain to reveal all manner of things to us, and we will know that it was God who revealed such things because glory will be given to God for the work. So, when we feel other things, God will make it completely known that it is he who is speaking to us through such feelings. We can feel sickness leave our bodies or shivers of OVERWHELMING joy and peace run up our spines and everywhere throughout!

**THOUGHTS**

God talks to us through our thoughts, from within or from the outside of our minds. John 14:26: "But the Comforter, which is the Holy Ghost, whom the Father will send in my name, he shall teach you all things, and bring all things to your remembrance, whatsoever I have said unto you." As Jesus says in John 14:23, Jesus and the Father will live inside believers as the Holy Ghost. My first encounter with God was his interaction with my thoughts. I was 13

55

years old in junior high school. A particular day, I had decided that I was too depressed to keep on living, and so, I had decided to kill myself after school, maybe when I got home. Personally, I had understanding of who God was because I went to a private Christian school, but I wasn't a convinced believer, nor had I experienced any teaching about why forgiveness was important. Nevertheless, I tested God. I don't remember praying to God. I believe I said to myself, "I'm going to give God one chance to prove he exists: I'll talk to a pastor at school; if God wants to save me, he'll make it happen when I talk to the pastor." I didn't tell my pastor/teacher that I was planning on killing myself, but I talked to him about all the emotions I was feeling, the hurts and sorrows, depression because of my family issues. He noticed that my life was lacking forgiveness, among other things, and he decided to talk to me about it. When he started praying for me after our chat, I felt a strange presence over the door of the classroom. It looked like the air was thick and moving. All of a sudden, I heard my own thoughts in my head speaking to me, but I wasn't the one speaking. God said to me, "Stephen, if you do not choose me, you shall surely die." The words of the thought were clear as day! The only way I could describe it was like someone strumming the "strings" of my brain from the outside like one would pluck a guitar. From that moment on, I was hooked and needed to seek out WHO that was! I could tell his presence was on the outside of my body, too. Later on in life, after I had truly accepted Christ as my savior, any other time I heard God speak to me directly through my thoughts like that, his voice welled up from inside my chest. He lives inside me, after all.

## SPIRITUAL GROANINGS

Another way that God speaks from inside of us is through "groanings and utterances." Romans 8:26:

"Likewise the Spirit also helpeth our infirmities: for we know not what we should pray for as we ought: but the Spirit itself maketh intercession for us with groanings which cannot be uttered." The King James Bible is very poetic, and in such, it is very descriptive. Paul is also a very pictorial author. When he uses words and analogies, he wants to describe whole stories in between the lines of the words he writes, in the pictures he's drawing for us. This will be evident in the Word of the Day, "ARMOR." When we look at Romans 8:26, "groanings which cannot be uttered" is SO descriptive. Groanings are low, barely audible sounds, but Paul then says that they cannot be uttered. What does that mean? If it's an actual sound, it should be able to be verbally spoken! Well, it is "spoken" inside of us, and I am certain that "cannot be uttered" actually means that these sounds are not actual words in human languages that have specific written meaning. If they were to be spoken out loud, they would not necessarily have any specific human verbal meanings or translations... Sound like anything we know? I believe that the "groanings" are praying in tongues through the Holy Spirit, God's spiritual language that wells up from within us. Consider something else that verbally groans, such as an animal or people. Living creatures literally just make sounds when groaning, but that sound describes an EMOTIONAL FEELING that is being experienced inside the groaner! Compared to the Holy Spirit, when he utters groanings inside of believers, he is "making intercession" of prayer in tongues inside us by uttering feelings to us as the vehicle of this special spiritual language! I'm almost certain that believers do the same thing when we verbally pray in the Spirit. Keep in mind what feelings you're experiencing when you're praying in tongues to God. See if this is true for you!

I can also share that I personally and often hear the utterance of tongues in my head. I'm not too sure if Romans 8:26 proves the instances of hearing tongues being spoken in the thoughts, but I know in my heart that this is the Holy Spirit speaking in me. To further depict the understanding of tongues, I'm reminded of a story that my pastor at the time told during a meeting. When she was younger, she asked God to teach her how to walk in the fullness of speaking in tongues. God basically said to her, "Speak out loud in praise, every descriptive word you can think of concerning Me. When you run out of words to say, KEEP GOING, speaking out in praise." This makes me understand that the words that the Holy Spirit utters is always coming from a place of truth and reverence for who God is. If you wonder if your heart is right when you pray in tongues, search your heart to find out if the reason why you are praying in tongues is to glorify God in love and adoration or to glorify yourself in vanity. (Another thing to note for clarification, speaking in tongues in the purpose of giving prayer and praise to God is not the same as the purpose of PROPHESYING in tongues to other people.)

It has come to my attention that there are some Christians who do not believe in the gift of speaking in tongues. Most people generally have this issue of believing if the tongues are real or fake, until they realize how deeply involved the Holy Spirit is within them. I used to believe that tongues were a misconception of the fact that God worked miracles through the Apostles, like in Acts 2:4-11. The Apostles were able to speak and be heard by the multitude each in their own language. The Holy Spirit worked this miracle, of which I would call "prophetic tongues," giving one the ability to speak a human language that is unknown to the speaker. Or perhaps this miracle was more profound than that; the Apostles could have been speaking in their Galilean language while the Holy Spirit made the multitude hear their own languages. Despite this particular miracle, I have come to find that the speaking of tongues that I wrote about above and the speaking of tongues that most people call "gibberish" can be found elsewhere in the Bible as the spiritual language of God.

In 1 Corinthians 14:1-2, Paul begins to set the tone for the rest of the chapter. "Follow after charity, and desire spiritual gifts, but rather that ye may prophesy. For he that speaketh in an unknown tongue speaketh not unto men, but unto God: for no man understandeth him; howbeit in the spirit he speaketh mysteries." The word "unknown" is an added word in translation that is not transliterated, yet is implied within the context of all of chapter 14, starting in verse 2 when it says, "no man understandeth him." The NASB says, "for no one understands." That is a definitive statement that can imply that literally no person on earth can understand through human means what is being said in such a tongue. The rest of the chapter talks about edifying the church with prophecies more than dealing with tongues. In some cases, like in verses 21 and 22, it can be thought of that human tongues are implied in the text, but this doesn't necessarily rule out the "gibberish" language at which much of today's modern church scoffs. Verse 4: "He that speaketh in an unknown tongue edifieth himself; but he that prophesieth edifieth the church." Any tongues that are spoken in the spirit towards God are used to build up the faith and spirit of one's self. Jude 1:20-21: "But ye, beloved, building up yourselves on your most holy faith, praying in the Holy Ghost, keep yourselves in the love of God, looking for the mercy of our Lord Jesus unto eternal life." Praying in the Holy Spirit is a thing in and of itself, outside of the edification/prophesying in a group setting. I ask then, what kind of other human languages would the Holy Spirit cause us to pray when we are alone with him? There would be no use of human languages in that sense of praying in the Spirit! (If you didn't catch what I did there, I used 1 Corinthians 14:2-4 to show that verbally speaking in an unknown tongue is the same as praying in the Spirit in Jude 1:20-21.)

Mark 16:17: "And these signs shall follow them that believe; In my name shall they cast out devils; they shall speak with new tongues;" When Jesus lists off the signs that believers will perform, he says, "they shall speak with NEW tongues." Does this refer to languages that are "new-to-them" but still exist in the world? Or does it mean "literally new" and never spoken before? One would argue that if Jesus wanted to make that distinction, he would have said, "they shall speak with tongues of other lands," but he leaves that open-ended. There is no denying that there is a heavenly language. 1 Corinthians 13:1 makes a distinction by saying, "Though I speak with the tongues of men and of angels," and Revelations 2:17b says, "To him that overcometh will I give to eat of the hidden manna, and will give him a white stone, and in the stone a new name written, which no man knoweth saving he that receiveth it." If God were to give a white stone with a new name to EVERY person in heaven, I believe that he'd run out of human-language names to give! He will obviously use his own special language to name his children. When we consider "new tongues" in Mark 16:17 and mash that with the understanding I first wrote about, thoughts and feelings that come out of each person's imagination MUST be verbalized in different ways because each person has completely unique thoughts, feelings, and imaginations. This is why so many Christians testify that when they speak tongues in the spirit, it is unlike any other person's tongues that they've heard before.

(I have a testimony to add here! These last four paragraphs were actually the last things I wrote in this book. This book was finished and ready to publish! I wrote about the verbalization of thoughts and feelings being equivalent to that of speaking in tongues in the spirit, but I had this pull in my heart to go back and explain why the "gibberish" tongues are pertinent. I prayed for God to prove me right about my claims, without any doubts, and then I would go back to explain more here as he'd enable me to do so. One Friday night during a Bible study, my current pastor was being led by the Spirit, as he always prefers to preach, and he said, "Who wants to learn how to speak in tongues?" It was such an awesome answer to my prayer because he confirmed a lot about what I've written above. He said, "When you're speaking to God in the spirit, speak out to him with your imagination. Let your words carry meaning from your heart. If you're thinking to yourself, 'Am I really speaking in tongues? Because I don't feel like I'm making sense,' then you're doing it right because your flesh does not understand the ways of the Spirit. Trust the moving of the Holy Spirit inside you." Trust me that I didn't want to change anything in this book unless it was absolutely necessary! I'm glad God led me to go back, though. With this confirmed understanding that emotional feelings are a spiritual language, it has solidified my stance in chapter 45, Possessions Vs. Oppressions of a Spirit-Filled Christian, in that demons' favorite ways to speak to people in order to deceive them is through sending thoughts and emotions that are based upon lies. A very smart friend once told me, "If ants can basically send each other wi-fi signals, why can't humans do the same?" I believe he's more correct than he realizes, and you have a lot to look forward to in finishing this book!)

## ENVIRONMENTAL SIGNS

God speaks to us through signs in the environment. Genesis 1:14-15: "And God said, Let there be lights in the firmament of the heaven to divide the day from the night; and let them be for signs, and for seasons, and for days and years: and let them be for lights in the firmament of the heaven to give light upon the earth: and it was so." Signs are meant to be read; "and let them be for signs," has been read in so many different ways by so many different religions of whom look to the sun, moon, and stars as figures from which to gain inspiration, revelation, and guidance. This only proves that taking God out of context does not only happen when people read his inspired writings; without being firmly rooted in God's heart and in his identity, knowing exactly WHEN he is talking to us, people can take the signs they see in the environment out of context as well! Just in Christian circles alone, some people specifically believe that blood moon events are evidences of the end times prophecies becoming fulfilled, yet they've made numerous claims about when the rapture will take place and have been incorrect every time. Paralleled with this happening, anointed ministers are able to tell us that Christ is returning soon, simply because the Holy Spirit is telling them.

Let's look at other modern examples of God possibly talking to us through the environment to give us signs of things to soon occur. August 21, 2017, a total solar eclipse followed a projected path that appeared to cut the USA in half. [3] What was happening in 2017? Without getting into citing lots of references of events that took place, I think that it is common knowledge that political uproar had developed after President Trump had taken office, elected in 2016 and entered office in the beginning of 2017, supposedly sparking social divide in our nation, although I personally feel that social divide was already taking place when President Obama was in office, as well as much earlier before him. Does a total eclipse cutting the USA in half mean that God was trying to warn us about social divide in our country? Only anointed individuals who have been blessed with that information by God can say. June 16, 2020, a massive dust storm blew from the Sahara Desert towards and reaching the Caribbean and some of the shores of Eastern United States. [4] Ten days later, swarms of locusts had plagued many areas in Easter Africa and the Middle East, threatening starvation upon millions of people whose food the locusts had eaten. [5] Are these events signs from God? Again, only those who are anointed and blessed with God's insight into the matters would be able to answer that question.

When we look to the Bible for clearer answers concerning signs and wonders occurring in the environment, we can find many examples where God announces his intentions for performing such actions. Exodus 9:1-7: "Then the LORD said unto Moses, Go in unto Pharaoh, and tell him, Thus saith the LORD God of the Hebrews, Let my people go, that they may serve me. For if thou refuse to let them go, and wilt hold them still, behold, the hand of the LORD is upon thy cattle which is in the field, upon the horses, upon the asses, upon the camels, upon the oxen, and upon the sheep: there shall be a very grievous murrain. And the LORD shall sever between the cattle of Israel and the cattle of Egypt: and there shall nothing die of all that is the children's of Israel. And the LORD appointed a set time, saying, To morrow the LORD shall do this thing in the land. And the LORD did that thing on the morrow, and all the cattle of Egypt died: but of the cattle of the children of Israel died not one. And Pharaoh sent, and, behold, there was not one of the cattle of the Israelites dead. And the heart of Pharaoh was hardened, and he did not let the people go." Nine more plagues after that, we know what happened to Israel and Egypt. Despite what happened afterward, my point is clear: God is always making his actions and intentions known concerning signs and wonders that he performs. This was also clear in the previously mentioned Exodus 19:9 when God told Moses to gather the elders of Israel because he was going to speak loudly from a thick cloud on the mountain so that Israel would believe Moses' words forever.

## MIRACLES

God speaks to believers AND non-believers alike using instances of miracles in order to reach out and build our faith. This is evident through many miracles that Jesus and the Apostles had performed. Miracles still happen today! Chances are, if you are a believer, you've already experienced a supernatural miracle. If you haven't, I challenge you to search the scriptures to see how God works miracles; pray for God to teach you how he can manifest such miracles in your life... Jesus will do all things for those who ask in faith through his name!

## CIRCUMSTANCES

God speaks to us through signs in personal circumstances. Circumstances include when other people are empowered to prophesy God's words to us, when we see triggers around us that spark memories of things God previously mentioned (such as seeing a number that reminds you to look up a verse in God's Word or remember why he made such a number significant to you), when we read the Bible, when we listen to music, and when we are blessed with abundance and increase.

Concerning my last point, I'd like to discuss reasons why God may not speak to us, and it most relates to the understanding of God speaking to us through blessings of abundance and increase, although, it can relate to any other way God would choose to speak to us as well. Hebrews 11:6: "But without faith it is impossible to please him: for he that cometh to God must believe that he is, and that he is a rewarder of them that diligently seek him." God may not speak to some because they have no faith that he exists. He may not speak because they do not diligently seek him. Romans 8:7-8: "Because the carnal mind is enmity against God: for it is not subject to the law of God, neither indeed can be. So then they that are in the flesh cannot please God." Remember that Paul talks about two laws in his teachings, saying in Romans 7:25: "I thank God through Jesus Christ our Lord. So then with the mind I myself serve the law of God; but with the flesh the law of sin." God may not speak to people because they are still carnal, living in the flesh and not by the Spirit. James 1:6-8: "But let him ask in faith, nothing wavering. For he that wavereth is like a wave of the sea driven with the wind and tossed. For let not that man think that he shall receive any thing of the Lord. A double minded man is unstable in all his ways."

So, if one's heart is not right before God, that is like a murderer asking God for provision of new firearms. God is not going to want to bless a sinner whose heart is not geared towards possibly having faith in receiving Christ because it does not build the kingdom of God. In fact, it destroys it. Mark 3:24: "And if a kingdom be divided against itself, that kingdom cannot stand." If such a sinner prayed and received for that which he prayed from God, that sinner would think that his life is pleasing to God, and he will not want to change his wicked ways. Murder is a heavy extreme, but all willingness to sin affects the faith that is present inside one's heart. So, we can use a different example and get the same outcome. If a thief kept getting caught by the police for robbing jewelry stores, but he consistently prayed to get set free and kept getting bailed out without major consequences, then he'd believe that God approved of his life of crime! If a lying pastor is preaching in a church, if God generally blesses that pastor's ministry, then he will believe that his level and effort of preaching is pleasing to God and won't change! But that will destroy God's kingdom as well because Christians will be brought up believing false doctrine. Concerning false prophets, although these next verses can be applied to anyone of whom does not adhere to the truth, remember Matthew 7:15-17: "Beware of false prophets, which come to you in sheep's clothing, but inwardly they are ravening wolves. Ye shall know them by their fruits. Do men gather grapes of thorns, or figs of thistles? Even so every good tree bringeth forth good fruit; but a corrupt tree bringeth forth evil fruit." God will not speak to such people through blessings of abundance and circumstances. He may speak to them in other ways if it's his plan to choose them by plucking them out of a sinful existence and calling them into holiness.

# CHAPTER EIGHTEEN: HABITS

"All the things you fill your life with habitually, they cannot fill the void that sin had created in your heart. Do not be ashamed that you are made as a habitual creature physically and spiritually. Become addicted to relationship with Me. I love you. -- Sincerely, God"

Habits are created and maintained by consistent behaviors and choices. Everything that is not based upon Christ, dead and resurrected, is based upon a lie. I used to condemn myself for having an addictive personality. Then I found out through constant study and revelations in teachings that addiction is normal. Addiction is a part of EVERY PERSON, physically and spiritually. Without addiction, we could not develop tools of discipline in our lives. The importance and severity related to addiction depends in what it is rooted. God told Joshua in Joshua 1:8, right before entering into the promised land, "This book of the law shall not depart out of thy mouth, but thou shalt meditate therein day and night, that thou mayest observe to do according to all that is written therein: for then thou shalt make thy way prosperous, and then thou shalt have good success."

"Meditation" upon scripture is an act of concentrating

on a subject or the very words of God. What does it take to become dedicated to meditation? There needs to be a clear vision, purpose, and goal behind why one meditates. It takes a consistent sacrifice of time devoted to setting and accomplishing goals that are related to the meditation. When we look at this one example of Joshua 1:8, the habit that Joshua will have developed was to meditate day and night on the book of the law with the purpose of memorizing and performing the law always, with the goal of pleasing God, and with a vision of gaining prosperity and success.

The same pattern can be found when Paul was sending encouragement to Timothy in 1 Timothy 4:14-16: "Neglect not the gift that is in thee, which was given thee by prophecy, with the laying on of the hands of the presbytery. Meditate upon these things [the gift]; give thyself wholly to them; that thy profiting may appear to all. Take heed unto thyself, and unto the doctrine; continue in them [the gift, considering himself, and adhering to the doctrine]: for in doing this thou shalt both save thyself, and them that hear thee."

Part of having good habits is founded on extreme desire to please the Lord. As believers in Christ are called to daily deny ourselves, pick up our crosses, and follow him (Luke 9:23), we consider it a joy to not conform to this world but to be transformed by the renewing of our minds (Romans 12:2). In doing so, we take the old void that sin left behind in our hearts and fill it with the Holy Spirit. We return to our previous state of being addicted to knowing and loving God.

# CHAPTER NINETEEN: RECEIVE

"The best part about God's will is that it isn't something that HAS to be enforced onto you or worked through you in order for it to happen. Sometimes it's just something that you receive because life is a gift. Yet again, Hebrews 11:6 says that we must have faith in order to please God. In defining faith, one must believe that he exists and also diligently seek him, but it's important to realize that being rewarded for these things also pleases him because he loves us. In order to receive, one must have faith (believe in him, choose him, and seek him), listen when he speaks, respond to what he says to DO or BE, and then have an attitude of humility and gratitude (which is the opposite of pride). Only after all of this will we have true peace in receiving gifts from God, starting with the most important gift of all: Christ."

I dare say that after the Fast, Hebrews 11:6 became one of my favorite verses. I repeated it often in the original quotes of my journaling of many Words because it touched so many different points. It will be repeated in the Sermon About Faith! For now, the point I'm touching upon is that rewarding his creation with an abundant life also pleases God (John 10:10). God also made our receipt of an eternal gift part of his law of the New Covenant. God is a generous provider; anything that compliments who God is also satisfies his laws and statutes. I'm suggesting that God also follows his own laws by which he commands us to follow. Because of his love for us and the high regard for following the law of his own heart, it pleased him to supply Christ so that we may choose him in order to become RESTORED.

# CHAPTER TWENTY: RESTORED

"This word means to be brought back to an original state of being. This begs the question, 'What was our original state?' It was perfection. Only God is perfect, so this means that God was a part of our original state from the get-go. It is now the same after believing in Christ. Galatians 2:20 says, 'I am crucified with Christ: nevertheless I live; yet not I, but Christ liveth in me: and the life which I now live in the flesh I live BY the FAITH of the Son of God, who loved me, and gave himself for me.' The 'faith' referred here can mean Christ's act of dying for us, but it is also affirming that while we're on earth, we must live out Christ's faith in the Spirit. All this to say that just like we are to replace our desires with his desires, we need to replace our faith WITH HIS FAITH to attain what we had originally lost."

Mankind started off perfect and blessed (Genesis 1:28), and he said that all he created was good (Genesis 1:31). After the fall of mankind, none were good except God (Mark 10:18). Concerning the passages of the Sermon on the Mount, Jesus says in Matthew 5:48, "Be ye therefore perfect, even as your Father which is in heaven is perfect." He used this one statement to highlight some teachings in chapter 5 (as well as all of chapters 6 and 7) to basically tell everyone how they are to be perfect like the Father is perfect. During his ministry, Jesus always taught referencing the scriptures, specifically the law of Moses and the writings of the prophets. Little did they understand, Christ was to become the fulfillment of the law so that all of those teachings on the mount could actually be attainable for us when we receive the Holy Ghost. When anyone learns the Old Covenant law, they will always be directed to Jesus. Galatians 3:24: "Wherefore the law was our schoolmaster to bring us unto Christ, that we might be justified by faith."

"Justified" means to be freed from the guilt and penalty of sin. Matthew 12:37: "For by thy words thou shalt be justified, and by thy words thou shalt be condemned." John 14:23: "Jesus answered and said unto him, If a man love me, he will keep my words: and my Father will love him, and we will come unto him, and make our abode with him." 1 John 3:23-24: "And this is his commandment, That we should believe on the name of his Son Jesus Christ, and love one another, as he gave us commandment. And he that keepeth his commandments dwelleth in him, and he in him. And hereby we know that he abideth in us, by the Spirit which he hath given us." Declaring Christ as Lord and having faith in him brings us to justification, that is, justifying our spirits. Why? When Jesus was crucified, he fulfilled the Old Covenant law; he performed THE ACT of justification. It is because of his faith in the words of the Father that he went to the cross and died for all mankind. John 1:33: "And I knew him not: but he that sent me to baptize with water, the same said unto me, Upon whom thou shalt see the Spirit descending, and remaining on him, the same is he which baptizeth with the Holy Ghost." When we believe in Christ, our spirits are baptized into his

Spirit, and the Spirit is the one who makes our bodies live, like Galatians 2:20 says. If he is the one who lives, it is like we are the ones who died on the cross, and we remain dead but alive in his Spirit.

Refer to Hebrews 11:6 again. So, if we are dead, what faith is it that pleases the Father? Matthew 3:17: "And lo a voice from heaven, saying, This is my beloved Son, in whom I am well pleased." It is Christ's faith that pleases the Father. I will expound upon this further in the Sermon About Faith later on in the book. For now, it's important to understand that Christ's faith has everything to do with restoring us into justification (being blameless like Adam was when he was created) and restoring our very nature of everything we do on earth to that of emulating the nature of the Holy Spirit. When we desire to be God's love towards people, it is Christ's faith inside us that causes us to be like that. When we follow every word that the Father tells us, we are empowered to follow his words BY the faith of Christ. This is yet another example of how Christ's yoke is easy and his burden is light! Never do we have to be tempted to pray like the man in Mark 9:24, "Lord, I believe; help thou my unbelief!" Often times, we pray to God, "Build my faith," as if we expect him to level us up like a character in a video game. As long as Christ is in us, our personal faith will build when we realize that Christ's faith is the worker of miracles in our lives, not our faith. Although Jesus says in Mark 9:23, "If thou canst believe, all things are possible to him that believeth," Jesus also says in John 14:13-14, "And whatsoever ye shall ask in my name, that will I do, that the Father may be glorified in the Son. If ye shall ask any thing in my name, I will do it." That tells me that anything is possible if we ask Christ to do it! He has the faith to do it; he IS the faith that restores us to our original nature; he IS our original nature!

# CHAPTER TWENTY-ONE: IDOLATRY

Exodus 20:3 "Thou shalt have no other gods before me." We may take this verse for granted, thinking, "Well of course! I don't worship Islam, Buddhism, Hinduism, etc. I'm a Christian and believe that Jesus died on the cross for my sins!" But what does your browser history at 3am say? What does your fourth burger-run in one day say? What does your habit to check your social media notifications say? What does your third cup of coffee in four hours say? What does that needle and bottle say? These are all negative things that many people can agree shouldn't be made into a god and worshipped over Elohim, and yet, <u>people worship the feelings that these objects and actions give us.</u> Let's go one step further in making a list of things that could be idols... What does your worship of money and success say? What does your idolization of a good job, a spouse, kids, a house with a white-picket fence, and a car that's paid off say? What does your pride in knowing a lot of the Bible more than other people say about idolatry? What about pride in the fact that SOMEHOW YOU are special BECAUSE you can exorcise demons and heal the sick, like the people Jesus referenced in Matthew 7:21-23?

There will be those who say, "Lord, Lord! Didn't we cast

out demons and heal the sick in your name?" And he will say, "Depart from me, for I never <u>KNEW</u> you." It will be because casting out demons and healing the sick will have become more important to them <u>than God</u>. When Abraham listened to God and almost sacrificed his son Isaac, Abraham didn't have to doubt or dismantle worshipping the fact that he was a father; having the title of "father" was not an idol to him. Abraham had no other gods (figuratively or physically) BEFORE Elohim. When God says "no other gods <u>before</u> me," he's not saying that you can still have your gods but that he has to be your priority before the other gods. He's saying to worship no other gods before him IN HIS PRESENCE! God is everywhere and he lives in the hearts of believers, so it's clear...worship NOTHING else except God. What are your idols? Sacrifice them to God and replace them with Christ.

# CHAPTER TWENTY-TWO: TESTIMONY

This usually just means "the story of the past that made you who you are today," but God wants to remind you that there's more to it. Your testimony is not only the story of your past, but it is a declaration of who you ARE and what you will become in the future. It is the EXAMPLE that you SHINE TO OTHERS. If your example is that you would LIKE to break the law in order to reach non-believers, you are teaching people that God is lawless, and you can taint perspectives of belief. If you share unbelief, that God WON'T heal certain diseases, living in fear of disease, you are declaring that God is powerless. Your testimony is what you are clothed in: are you naked in shame, condemnation, and guilt; or are you clothed in righteousness of <u>full surrender in Christ</u>? You don't need to feel burdened in "convincing" people of the truth of which you're living out; all you have to do is live confidently in the truth and your identity IN that truth. Always be confidently ready to share your testimony to others; continuously live your testimony out towards others.

1 Peter 3:13-17: "And who is he that will harm you, if ye be followers of that which is good? But and if ye suffer for righteousness' sake, happy are ye: and be not afraid of their

terror, neither be troubled; but sanctify the Lord God in your hearts: and be ready always to give an answer to every man that asketh you a reason of the hope that is in you with meekness and fear: having a good conscience; that, whereas they speak evil of you, as of evildoers, they may be ashamed that falsely accuse your good conversation in Christ. For it is better, if the will of God be so, that ye suffer for well doing, than for evil doing."

# CHAPTER TWENTY-THREE: PROVISION

God is our provider. Simple. It doesn't matter the quality of life we have, whether we are poor enough where nobody would blame us for pan-handling or rich enough to own a whole city. The one thing God is FOCUSED on providing us is the means of eternal salvation (which he provided in Christ's sacrifice) and the experiences of faith that lead us to choosing Christ. God is faithful and loving enough to care about even the smallest creatures' needs, so how much more does he want to care for our needs? But don't be confused about God's end result and plan. On the other side of the coin, God calls us to help people (heal the sick, feed the hungry, clothe and house the poor) just like the good Samaritan parable found in Luke 10:25-37. In this sense, because we carry his Spirit, we are partakers of the experiences he provides to other people in order to grow faith in those people, reaching out in a physical way to those who are stuck in a carnal mindset. The goal is to eventually encourage the carnally minded to learn how to be spiritually minded in pursuit of God's truth in Christ.

God cares for our needs. He is Adonai, the God of more than enough. He put two humans in the middle of an excessive realm of overflowing abundance. Then he said,

"Be blessed and multiply." Some people think that it's frivolous to suggest that God cares about what kind of toothbrush and toothpaste I should buy at the store when there are children dying of cancer or hunger all around the world. Maybe he cares more about the fact that I'd ask him anything and desire to know what he'd suggest, and then maybe he cares more about the dying children than about me asking about my dental needs. But the thing about God is that he's allowed to care about EVERYTHING! He made everything, after all. God is the best realist! His will flows into this world, and he knows how to make everything work towards the good of those who love him. (Romans 8:28)

# CHAPTER TWENTY-FOUR: CHARITY

This is the perfect word to occur right after "provision," as we are part of the spiritual kingdom that reaches out to the carnally-minded. The definition according to the dictionary is, "The voluntary giving of help, typically in the form of money, to those in need." [6] The Bible definitions are so vast, but I'd like to focus on the definition of "charity" that means "love," found in 1 Corinthians chapter 13. I asked God once why the KJV Bible says "charity" there instead of "love." The answer that was given to me was that love is pointless in its purpose if it is not given to others. In reading 2 Corinthians 9:7, we find that the same is true of "charity" if it is not done out of love. "Every man according as he purposeth in his heart, so let him give; not grudgingly, or of necessity: for God loveth a cheerful giver." The only way one can give cheerfully without having a grudge about it (or feel like one is forced to give) is if one has love. The best part about this verse is "purposeth in his heart," because it allows us to focus on Christ's heart that we are supposed to have. If we are supposed to have Christ's heart, we can insert a new understanding and read the verse like this: "Every man, according as God gives purpose from His heart, should be a cheerful and loving giver." We have God's love; we are God's love towards others. We are ready to provide physically to others what God will use to grow faith in their hearts that will eventually lead people to accepting Christ in their hearts. It's not just another job to spread the truth of the Gospel that rescues people from shame with the blood of Jesus. It's who we are!

# CHAPTER TWENTY-FIVE: ARMOR

Earlier in this work, I described a unique habit of Paul the Apostle when he wrote his letters to various churches and brothers in Christ. Paul's habits included referencing Old Testament characters and describing how their actions foreshadow the events that would lead to Jesus. Another habit was also that of writing run-on thoughts, in which case, if you see the beginning of a sentence start with any words like, "so," "then," "also," "therefore," et cetera, then you better make sure to read the verses that appear before those occurrences so that you can gain more complete context of his thoughts. The same is true when he wrote in a way that the translators had to end verses with colons; everything after a colon is meant to explain a point previously made before it. The major habit I previously mentioned, though, is that Paul often wrote visual descriptions within simple phrases of things that people wouldn't often think in a deeply visual way, drawing pictures in between the lines. This is how I viewed these occurrences to "crack his code:" take the FUNCTION of the descriptive object and apply that function to the subject of which it's describing. One of my favorite examples of this is when Paul talks about the Armor of God. I will outline this descriptive code about the Armor of God in this section.

There's a point in life where we have to choose to protect ourselves (making responsible decisions) and where we simply trust that we're protected. Well, I ask, why do we have to shift mindsets? The point is that we shouldn't, that our "responsible decision" is to be rooted in the Holy Spirit. These two mindsets of fight or flight are compared and contrasted in Ephesians chapter 6. We aren't the ones who are running away, but we aren't the ones fighting either! Jesus is! Verses 13 to 17 tell us how to overcome the world with the Armor of God.

Ephesians 6:11-20 NASB: "Put on the full armor of God, so that you will be able to stand firm against the schemes of the devil. For our struggle is not against flesh and blood, but against the rulers, against the powers, against the world forces of this darkness, against the spiritual forces of wickedness in the heavenly places. Therefore, take up the full armor of God, so that you will be able to resist on the evil day, and having done everything, to stand firm. Stand firm therefore, having belted your waist with truth, and having put on the breastplate of righteousness, and having strapped on your feet the preparation of the gospel of peace; in addition to all, taking up the shield of faith with which you will be able to extinguish all the flaming arrows of the evil one. And take the helmet of salvation and the sword of the Spirit, which is the word of God. With every prayer and request, pray at all times in the Spirit, and with this in view, be alert with all perseverance and every request for all the saints, and pray in my behalf, that speech may be given to me in the opening of my mouth, to make known with boldness the mystery of the gospel, for which I am an ambassador in chains; that in proclaiming it I may speak boldly, as I ought to speak."

So, wearing our armor is being rooted in these six points in Christ which are actually visual representations that describe what we are to do and be:

## BELT OF TRUTH

Having a love for God's truth and operating in it is like a belt holding your clothes in place so that you aren't standing in shame. When I think of shame, I think of Adam and Eve in the garden of Eden, naked and unashamed. When they gained the knowledge of good and evil, they knew that they were naked, and they became ashamed in their sin. God covered them, which represents what God did through Christ's sacrifice so that none who will believe in Christ Jesus would ever live with shame. The truth of Christ covers our shame like a belt keeps clothing from falling off, which would cause us to be naked and vulnerable. So, in everything you do and are, seek and live out the truth of Christ.

## BREASTPLATE OF RIGHTEOUSNESS

A breastplate covers our bodies' vital organs besides the head. These vital organs represent in the natural what our spirits represent in the spirit realm. The breastplate is our relationship with the Holy Spirit after believing in Jesus Christ and his sacrifice. Believing in Jesus and making him Lord over our lives makes us righteous. That righteousness protects us from being owned by anyone other than God, as well as protects the core of who we are from deserving death.

## ARMORED SHOES

"Shoes of readiness that comes from the Gospel of peace," as the KJV says. Feet are what you literally stand on. They represent what you stand FOR. The rest of the body is important, as well as the armor that's attached to those body parts, but it's important to understand that the feet are THE body parts that are ALWAYS in contact with the ground, which represents this physical world. So, having shoes allows you to be at peace no matter what physical tribulation you may step on, as opposed to not wearing shoes while you step on a Lego or stub your toe. If the true gospel IS our shoes, we are ready to walk through anything this world has that would try to make us stumble. If the enemy can trip us up in our doctrines of the gospel, that is like wearing shoes with holes in the bottom of them. When we walk, we will not be at peace. Be led by the Spirit in studying what that true gospel of Christ is!

## SHIELD OF FAITH

Faith IS belief. How does one believe? "Faith comes by hearing, and hearing by the Word of God." When we hear God's words in our lives, they are usually happening during physical experiences that he provides to us directly or through those who have the Holy Spirit. So how does Faith shield us? In these three ways: first, faith is needed in order to attain God's promise of salvation through Christ; second, we have these memories of God speaking to us, making himself real to us. Hold onto those memories like they are real and can be held in your hand because they DID HAPPEN to you! This is YOUR proof for yourself that nobody can take away from you no matter how many fiery arrows someone shoots at you to try to make you doubt God. Third, just like a warrior in battle, a shield can be used to slap an enemy down; in this case, God can work his faith through us to provide a tangible experience to unbelievers so that they themselves now have something to hold onto in faith. When we adhere to these examples of faith, we are shielded from all sides.

## HELMET OF SALVATION

A helmet protects the head, brain, etc. The head can be thought of to represent the mind in this depiction. So, the helmet of salvation represents a mindset that protects us from believing in specific lies that say we aren't salvageable because we are too sinful and unworthy. We WERE as filthy rags, but after believing in Christ, salvation is given freely to us from the Father! This mindset snuffs out self-condemnation and shame, starting over with God's forgiveness. Satan will attack our minds the most because if he can convince us that what we believe is false, we may end up denying Christ. Some say that because of John 10:28-29 (among other verses) that no Christian is able to lose salvation once believing in Christ. When we look at the transliteration from the Greek of the word "pluck" in these verses, it means, "harpazo," which is to say, "to seize, carry off by force." [7] So, when it says, "neither shall any man pluck them out of my hand," and, "no man is able to pluck them out of my Father's hand," it can be read as, "nobody is able to forcibly take God's sheep." Those with this position will say, "A Christian is part of that 'nobody' group of those who can't forcibly steal themselves away from God." But when a converting Christian denies Christ, it is not by force, but by willful decision. Therefore, salvation is indicative upon whether Christians willfully remain to be sheep by continuing to believe in Christ. Romans 8:14: "For as many as are led by the Spirit of God, they are the sons of God." When Christians choose to not renew their minds nor be led by the Spirit, they are still saved because they believe in Christ (and believing on Christ invites the Holy Spirit to baptize our spirits), but the path of living life controlled/led by the flesh will bring such a Christian to a final decision-point where a life experience will require him/her to choose physical life by denying Christ or to choose physical death by proclaiming Christ. We see it happen all the time in society! I believe that the devil knows about this "plucking" loophole where evil people who shoot up villages, malls, or schools will say to a person, "Deny your God, or I will shoot you!" When the devil can trick you into making the choice of denying Christ, you've done what he could never do. Matthew 16:25: "For whosoever will save his life shall lose it: and whosoever will lose his life for my sake shall find it."

It wouldn't be right to say all of this without showing examples of people in the Bible, gaining and losing their place in the kingdom of God. The first example comes from the parable of the unforgiving servant that Jesus told of which I mentioned earlier. (Matthew 18:21-35) Peter asked Jesus how many times he should forgive his brother. Jesus basically said that he should never stop forgiving his brother. Then he proceeded to tell his parable. In verse 26, the first servant fell down and begged the ruler for patience in repaying his debt. The ruler had compassion on the servant and FORGAVE him the debt. In verses 32-34, the ruler was angry with that servant for not forgiving a debt of another servant, so he sent him to prison with "the tormentors" until the ORIGINAL DEBT was paid. This parable would not typically be considered as a matter of fact in order to prove my original point, EXCEPT that verse 35 says, "So likewise shall my heavenly Father do also unto you, if ye from your hearts forgive not every one his brother their trespasses." This solidifies the fact that even though this was just a parable, this is how things work in God's kingdom.

This parable was told during the time when everyone was still under the Old Covenant laws because Jesus had not yet died and rose again. So, we need more examples during the New Covenant to further this point that loss of position is possible. Acts 5:1-11 tells the story of Ananias and Sapphira. In Acts chapter 4, a church of believers out of 5000 converted Jews began a new custom in their congregation. They each sold their land and gave the profit of such to the apostles so that the apostles would supply all of the church's needs with that money. Acts 4:31-33 shows that all those who were in this church received the same experience with the Holy Spirit upon believing in Christ. "And when they had prayed, the place was shaken where they were assembled together; and they were ALL filled with the Holy Ghost, and they spake the word of God with boldness. And the multitude of them that believed were of one heart and of one soul: neither said any of them that ought of the things which he possessed was his own; but they had all things common. And with great power gave the apostles witness of the resurrection of the Lord Jesus: and great grace was upon them all." So, if anyone was a part of this particular church, he/she had received the Holy Spirit. The fact that Ananias and Sapphira were a part of this church, involved in the eventual custom of selling their land, and giving the money to the apostles meant that they had the Holy Spirit from their original experience after believing in Christ (because ALL were filled with the Holy Ghost). But in Acts 5:3, we see that Satan gave them the idea to lie about keeping back part of the profits for themselves. "Why hath Satan filled thine heart to lie to the Holy Ghost?" (The transliteration of the word "filled" in the Greek is "pleroo" which can mean, "to supply liberally," or, "to carry into effect." [8] So, no, Satan did not fill Ananias and Sapphira with HIMSELF, but that of the whisperings of temptations to commit sin.) They were both separately struck down for their spiritual rebellion by the power of God. Christians are not supernaturally judged by God for their actions and yet capable of retaining the Holy Spirit inside them because a kingdom divided against itself cannot stand. (Mark 3:24) Therefore, I conclude that Ananias and Sapphira willfully denied the Holy Spirit with their lie.

Revelation chapter 3 has a couple of good examples of what will happen in the end times, as stated to some churches concerning their need for correction. Concerning the point of the fact that those who deny Christ will deny salvation that they've attained, verses 5, 8, 10, and 11 help me raise this strong point to those who believe otherwise: I ask, "If those who become true Christians will never lose their salvation, then what is the point of keeping God's word and 'not denying' his name?" Revelation 3:5: "He that overcometh, the same shall be clothed in white raiment; and I will not blot out his name out of the book of life, but I will confess his name before my Father, and before his angels." In order for the name to be blotted OUT of the book of life, it had to originally be written there by receiving Christ as Lord. Verse 8: "I know thy works: behold, I have set before thee an open door, and no man can shut it: for thou hast a little strength, and hast kept my word, and hast not denied my name." Verses 10 and 11: "Because thou hast kept the word of my patience, I also will keep thee from the hour of temptation, which shall come upon all the world, to try them that dwell upon the earth. Behold, I come quickly: hold that fast which thou hast, that no man take thy crown." The transliteration of "crown" in the Greek is "stephanos," which means, "a mark of royal or exalted rank." [9] What is it that they are to "hold fast" to which they have in order for man to not take away their mark of royalty? Our royal inheritance as the seed of Abraham is attained from our faith in Christ. They will try to make you give up your faith! Keep on your helmet of salvation by always having this mindset that NEVER gives up believing in Christ!

**THE SWORD OF THE SPIRIT**

Ephesians 6 says that the sword of the Spirit is the Word

of God. Anything that God says, whether written or spoken, is a sword that cuts through the lies of the enemy. If we back up everything that we are with the words from God, the enemy cannot stand. The logic of false doctrines becomes destroyed. A perfect example of this is when Jesus was led into the wilderness for 40 days and nights to be tempted by Satan. Every time Satan proposed a new temptation, the only defense Jesus used was the words of God from scripture. "IT IS WRITTEN...IT IS WRITTEN...IT IS WRITTEN!" He used no other means of battling Satan. This is our most powerful example because it shows that WE are FULLY CAPABLE of withstanding Satan in the same way!

Prayer is also mentioned as being a part of the Helmet of Salvation and the Sword of the Spirit. We use prayer to know God in salvation and communion. We use prayer to deliver the sword against the enemy no matter where evil is happening. Speak God's words BOLDLY. Pray to God BOLDLY. A sword does not swing in vain!

# CHAPTER TWENTY-SIX: HABITATION

Psalm 91:5-6 says that we should not be afraid of a large list of evils. How does one attain this fearless state? Verses 9 and 10 answer this question. "Because thou hast made the LORD, which is my refuge, even the most High, <u>thy habitation</u>; there shall no evil befall thee, neither shall any plague come nigh <u>thy dwelling</u>." When we make God our habitation, we have nothing to fear. This raises a lot of questions because it seems like our physical dwelling place is what's being referenced here, but it's specifically not. What are "we?" "We" are spirits. Where do our spirits dwell? Inside our bodies. The definition of "habitation" is "the state or process of living in a particular place." [10] If our state of living is supposed to be "in the LORD," this correlates directly with Romans chapter 8 where we are to walk by the Spirit and not by the flesh. The fun part here is that we can play with the definitions of the root words to get a clearer understanding of what living in the Spirit actually IS! The root of "habitation" is "habitat," which means, "the <u>natural</u> home or environment of an animal, plant, or organism." [11] In this case, we'll just say that our spirits are the "organisms" here in this very physical definition. The root of "natural" is "nature," of which both words have multiple definitions relating to physical things. But one definition of "nature" sticks out to me: when it is used in the phrase "in my nature," as in to say, "my originally created purpose," or, "how I was made originally." Since our nature was perfect before the Fall, and since sin changed our nature to be concerned with life in the flesh, in order to make our habitation in God's Spirit, we must be changed to reflect that of who God is, his "nature" or state of being. The only way this can happen is by believing and accepting Christ's sacrifice and then being changed by relationship with God, diligently seeking him forever. When you live in a House that supplies your every need, physically and spiritually, you never have to leave!

# CHAPTER TWENTY-SEVEN: PRAISE

"We live in the nature of who God is. What it looks like is continuous praise to God in everything that happens. This is what we do when our spirits live in his Spirit, praising God for eternity. For he inhabits the praises of his people! (Psalm 22:3)"

I was once praising God in worship music; one song that came up on the list was "Even When It Hurts" by Hillsong United. When the lyrics came up, "I will only sing your praise," God RUSHED me with a word! He said to me, "Whenever you sing this song, I want you to replace these words with, 'I will only LIVE your praise.'" Praising God in reverence does not just happen in worship music. We are meant to praise God with ALL our actions, big and small! Is what you're doing giving God glory? If not, then why? Eternity in heaven is going to be full of praising God. We are his children NOW, so we should be praising God with ALL our actions NOW! I'll let these next verses speak for themselves.

Hebrews 13:15: "By him therefore let us offer the sacrifice of praise to God continually, that is, the fruit of our lips giving thanks to his name."

Psalm 34:1b: "I will bless the LORD at all times: his

praise shall continually be in my mouth."

Psalm 150:6: "Let every thing that hath breath praise the LORD. Praise the LORD."

1 Corinthians 4:5: "Therefore judge nothing before the time, until the Lord come, who both will bring to light the hidden things of darkness, and will make manifest the counsels of the hearts: and then shall every man have praise of God."

1 Corinthians 6:20: "For ye are bought with a price: therefore glorify God in your body, and in your spirit, which are God's."

(Also refer to the list of things Paul instructs to do in Romans chapter 12 as a fulfillment of presenting our bodies as living sacrifices, as Romans 12:1 states.)

# CHAPTER TWENTY-EIGHT: AGREEMENT

"Praying in agreement with each other is an important gesture within the church, but remember that agreement with each other is not the goal in prayer; it's having our hearts be in agreement with God's heart. When we pray and when we ask others to specifically pray for something, are we absolutely sure that we're praying for God's will? In every situation, pray for God to align your heart with his heart and teach you how to pray, then pray for others to be in agreement with God's heart when he tells you how to pray. (Refer to Romans 8:26 again concerning instruction on how to pray.)"

Matthew 18:19-20: "Again I say unto you, That if two of you shall agree on earth as touching any thing that they shall ask, it shall be done for them of my Father which is in heaven. For where two or three are gathered together in my name, there am I in the midst of them." "In my name" is not a magic phrase that suddenly allows you to receive anything you want. "In my name" can be better described pictorially as an army that's ready for battle, armed together under the same "banner" of what it means to be in Christ. Amos 3:3: "Can two walk together, except they be agreed?"

Likewise, can two or three (or many) Christians be gathered together in "battle" under the same banner of Christ and not be in agreement with the Leader of the army?

I pray that more Christians around the world become revived in agreement with each other and with the heart of God in one body through Christ!

# CHAPTER TWENTY-NINE: REVELATION

Receiving a revelation is a direct impartation of words from God, as the Greek word "Rhema" is defined as "a specific word for an individual," or simply understood as "an utterance." [12] God's "rhema" is directly related to the Sword of the Spirit. It is an IMMEDIATE word that interacts with our willingness to perform "shama," which is a Hebrew word that basically means "listen and obey." [13] If you've ever felt God give you knowledge about an action and URGE you to do it, this is what that is. Revelations could be just receiving knowledge alone, but God rarely tells us something if he doesn't want us to APPLY his words to our lives. The ability of receiving revelations and performing God's desires is surrounded by the heart posture of "The Fear of the Lord."

Acting out the instructions of his words is the fulfillment of our faith in him and what he says. Listening to instructions includes following them. We went over all the ways that God talks to us in the Word of the Day, "LISTENING." Like I said, REVELATION is the purpose of why we should listen to God in the first place. Faith in God is FILLED with actions that prove our heart to him because faith without works is dead. If we love him, we will do his commandments. This is the whole reason why I even began to write this book. He SHOOK my life with revelations of truth that I just can't keep to myself! Ultimately, the purpose of why I do this is to glorify God IN YOUR SPIRITS with the truth of Christ, that the kingdom of God would grow INSIDE YOU!

# CHAPTER THIRTY: THE FEAR OF THE LORD

Proverbs 1:7 says, "The fear of the LORD is the beginning of knowledge: but fools despise wisdom and instruction." This "fear" is directly related to our ability to receive and carry out instructions. I had an understanding of the fear of the Lord as, "a fear of ever being able to disappoint God," but God showed me that the fear of the Lord is more like a Godly "fear" or "reverence" in that of being persistently ready to make sure God receives ALL the glory in everything we do, including when his Holy Spirit urges us into action. "Fear" is used as a physically descriptive word of a spiritual action. True love casts out all fear; there is no fear in relationship with God. Just like we did with Paul's writings, using the physical description of "fear," imagine the responsive action behind someone who has <u>actual</u> fear: see a spider and run away; about to fall off a ledge and grab onto something for dear life; gun shots fired and duck/run; etc. Our heart posture of always giving God the glory in everything needs to exist in us like a readiness that is a second-nature response, just like fear causes a second-nature response! In this heart posture, we are not focused on our own issues or motives, enough so that we can hear God clearer and enact his will with extreme confidence and IMMEDIATE readiness when he tells us to do or be something.

# CHAPTER THIRTY-ONE: AFFLICT THE SOUL

The Day of Atonement is a holy day that Israel was instructed to keep. In Leviticus 16:29-31 and Numbers 29:7-12, you'll find that "afflict the soul" is specifically mentioned as a statute. A statute is the type of law that simply exists, much like the law of gravity. So, this mindset of afflicting one's soul is necessary and pleasing to God in this time of atonement. But what does it mean to afflict the soul? "Afflict" means to cause mental or physical pain or suffering,[14] so we can assume that this phrase has something to do with spiritual suffering. Isaiah 64:7 describes a time when God was silent because of iniquities, and verse 12 says, "Wilt thou refrain thyself for these things, O Lord? Wilt thou hold thy peace, and afflict us very sore?" This is a good description of spiritual suffering, being disconnected from God, but it is not the same as afflicting our own souls. This phrase is only found in the King James Version Bible, and in many other verses where "afflict the soul" is found, it's translated as "humble yourself," or better related as "deny yourself." Yet, there's more to it. The characteristics of afflicting the soul can be found in a few verses, such as Ezra 8:21 where it's said to be used to seek God's directions and provisions. Numbers 30:13 mentions that afflicting the soul can be made in an oath. Isaiah 58:5 relates it to fasting, which can relate to the observance of the Day of Atonement. Isaiah 58:13-14 fortifies this with characteristics of how he wants them to observe this fasting. "If thou turn away thy foot from the sabbath, from doing thy pleasure on my holy day; and call the sabbath a delight, the holy of the Lord, honourable; and shalt honour him, not doing thine own ways, nor finding thine own pleasure, nor speaking thine own words: Then shalt thou delight thyself in the Lord; and I will cause thee to ride upon the high places of the earth, and feed thee with the heritage of Jacob thy father: for the mouth of the Lord hath spoken it."

We can now attribute all of these characteristics with what pleases God on the Day of Atonement! It's important to remember that Christ's sacrifice replaces and fulfills all atonement for our sins, making EVERY DAY HOLY since we can receive forgiveness whenever we decide to inevitably believe and seek relationship with God. The law has been fulfilled in Christ. Without possessing the above characteristics, the "works of the flesh" found in Galatians 5:19-21 are likely to be how one lives. But HAVING all of these characteristics of denying one's own pleasures, own ways, speaking one's own words, and delighting one's self in what pleases the Lord, manifests the fruits of the Spirit found in Galatians 5:22-23. The next verses of Galatians 5:24-25 define the true meaning of "afflict the soul" in relation to the characteristics of the actions. "And they that are Christ's have crucified the flesh with the affections and lusts. If we live in the Spirit, let us also walk in the Spirit."

"Afflict the soul" means to have everything in us that has to do with carnality die so that all that's left is God. All of this relates to these words of the day: restored; carnality;

called to be holy; and righteous. While Israel was reminded about this every year, celebrating the Day of Atonement, we are called to be this way every day forever, to forever deny ourselves for the sake of glorifying the Father through Jesus Christ.

# CHAPTER THIRTY-TWO: LIMITATIONS

"The only limitation in us is lack of faith. There are no limitations in real faith."

Luke 7:1-10 is the story of the centurion who went to Jesus to heal his servant, but this man was special, in that he made Jesus marvel at his faith. Oh, how I'd love to hear Jesus say to me, "YOU ARE FULL OF FAITH!" This story showed us that all Jesus had to do is say the word no matter where he was, and the world obeyed him, even from afar! The spirit world is not limited by space and time!

Mark 11:23-24: "For verily I say unto you, That whosoever shall say unto this mountain, Be thou removed, and be thou cast into the sea; and shall not doubt in his heart, but shall believe that those things which he saith shall come to pass; he shall have whatsoever he saith. Therefore I say unto you, What things soever ye desire, when ye pray, believe that ye receive them, and ye shall have them."

If you believe that you've already received what you've prayed, you receive your prayers! This is a faith that REQUIRES us to be dead to our senses because we live by faith and not by sight. It requires us to live for purpose on purpose! It requires us to know that WE aren't the ones who perform miracles; it's Christ who does the real work of faith from inside us! The fruits of the Spirit and the gifts of the Spirit do not occur outside of God's love and his will; therefore, our faith requires us to be God's love and identity towards others and towards ourselves. In true freedom in our identities in Christ, we will have no limitations!

# CHAPTER THIRTY-THREE: MEEKNESS

Matthew 5:5: "Blessed are the meek: for they shall inherit the earth."

The meaning of "meek," according to a general dictionary is, "quiet, gentle, and obedient." [15] The Bible is similar in definition, but it goes a little deeper. We have to ask some questions about meekness to clarify why it is a fruit of the Spirit, described in Galatians 5:23. To whom is meekness portrayed? What does meekness look like? What purposes does meekness fulfill?

Titus 3:1-2: "Put them in mind to be subject to principalities and powers, to obey magistrates, to be ready to every good work, to speak evil of no man, to be no brawlers, but gentle, shewing all meekness unto all men." This answers that we should be meek towards all men. The purpose of this is shown in Titus 3:14. "And let ours also learn to maintain good works for necessary uses, that they be not unfruitful." All of these good works towards men shows that the purpose of being meek, among other things, is to grow the seeds of the gospel in others. As a fruit of the Spirit, it is part of our outward testimony towards others that the Spirit leads us. This answers most things off that bat, but what does meekness necessarily look like? Are we supposed to submit to all people around us like we're weak cowards? Heavens, no!

This section of scripture in 2 Corinthians 10:1-11 gives a good account of what it looks like to be meek towards men: "Now I Paul myself beseech you by the meekness and gentleness of Christ, who in presence am base among you, but being absent am bold toward you: but I beseech you, that I may not be bold when I am present with that confidence, wherewith I think to be bold against some, which think of us as if we walked according to the flesh. For though we walk in the flesh, we do not war after the flesh: (for the weapons of our warfare are not carnal, but mighty through God to the pulling down of strong holds;) casting down imaginations, and every high thing that exalteth itself against the knowledge of God, and bringing into captivity every thought to the obedience of Christ; and having in a readiness to revenge all disobedience, when your obedience if fulfilled. [A "readiness to revenge all disobedience" means to fight an evil deed with a good deed of your obedience to God, in this context.] Do ye look on things after the outward appearance? If any man trust to himself that he is Christ's, let him of himself think this again, that, as he is Christ's, even so are we Christ's. [We are no different than the one to whom we are to show meekness.] For though I should boast somewhat more of our authority, which the Lord hath given us for edification, and not for your destruction, I should not be ashamed: that I may not seem as if I would terrify you by letters. For his letters, say they, are weighty and powerful; but his bodily presence is weak, and his speech contemptible. [This is Paul talking about himself.] Let such an one think this, that, such as we are in word by letters when we are absent, such will we be also in deed [actions] when we are present." Here, we see a clear distinction between the message that

Paul tries to get across in letters as opposed to the tone he spoke with his words in front of people. The point of this was to not steer some people away from his words just because of the way he sounded, but when he was with those people, he put his words to action in their lives. So, it's understandable that meekness is a form of peace derived from humility, in a sense that one is not ruled by his/her emotions in the heat of the moment or at all. If one doesn't have humility, what would be the motivation to reach others with the gospel message?

In the beginning of these passages, Paul points out that this meekness and gentleness are of Christ. Using Christ as an example, we see in his ministry that he was bold in his mission yet compassionate towards all kinds of people. The one time recorded that it seemed like Jesus was quite forceful was when he fashioned a whip and drove out all of the merchants and animals from the temple. He was bold to defend his Father's house. Like him, we are to be bold in defending our Father's kingdom, that is, the truth of his words. Yet, with almost every encounter Jesus had, he was calm, cool, and collected, able to show mercy to sinners and tax collectors, and able to dismantle the arguments of the Pharisees without resorting to carnally-driven, emotional reactions. A secondary definition for "meekness" in some verses is "humility." [16] Hebrews 2:9 and Philippians 2:7 both describe how Jesus was equal to God and yet humbled himself to that of a human so that he could become our sacrifice for sins. His authority did not diminish, though, just his position.

So, in his example we have a strong clue as to the nature of meekness. Jesus was meek to men, showing love and compassion to them because he loved the Father and was humble towards him. We see descriptions of this in Zephaniah chapters 2 and 3. Zephaniah 2:3: "Seek ye the

LORD, all ye meek of the earth, which have wrought his judgement; seek righteousness, seek meekness: it may be ye shall be hid in the day of the LORD's anger." "Wrought" in this verse means to do, to make, or more accurately, to perform the Lord's judgements. These meek described in the verse are to seek righteousness and then MORE meekness. As we've looked closer, this meekness is a humility that is not surrendered towards men, but towards God.

The rest of the chapter talks about what God will do to those societies who were not humble/meek, and verse 10 explains why. "This shall they have for their pride, because they have reproached and magnified themselves against the people of the LORD of hosts." Zephaniah 3:1-2 talks about a particular "rejoicing city that dwelt carelessly." "Woe to her that is filthy and polluted, to the oppressing city! She obeyed not the voice; she received not correction; she trusted not in the LORD; she drew not near to her God." These verses show that the opposites of meekness are pride, bringing ourselves above God's purposes, not obeying God's voice, not receiving correction, nor trusting or seeking God. Therefore, we are to do these things in our walk with God, and the fruit of the Spirit which comes out of us in the form of meekness will be a loving and gentle demeanor towards men because we are loving and humble towards the Father in these things. The Holy Spirit causes us to be meek the more we draw closer to him.

# CHAPTER THIRTY-FOUR: WISDOM

"Wisdom is acquiring knowledge AND having the ability to use that knowledge. It requires discernment of what is true, the ability to hear this truth (whether it be information that's stored into you over time due to experience, or if it be something that God tells you in the moment), faith to BELIEVE the knowledge you possess, and the ability to implement this information in real life or inside of you. It's possible to have wisdom in some things as opposed to other things. (Refer to Exodus 35:30-33, where God filled Bezaleel with wisdom, understanding, and knowledge in all manner of workmanship so that they could create the tented tabernacle.) It's also possible for God to implant an umbrellaed wisdom into you like he did for Solomon, but as we see with the example of Solomon, wisdom is useless and wicked if it is used contrary to God's will. Seek God's wisdom and direction in everything you're currently dealing with before trying to fulfill a NEED of gaining ALL his wisdom at once. Be faithful with the little knowledge you have right now so that God can grant you more wisdom in the future."

When I was writing this Word, the parable of the talents came to mind from Matthew 25:14-30. The story starts off with a master who gave three servants three different amounts of talents or currency. A talent was a measurement of precious metals, like gold and silver, that weighed about 75 pounds. [17] To one he gave five talents; to another he gave two talents; to the last he gave one talent. These certain amounts were given based upon each servant's ability to manage them. I liked to think that "talents" is an excellent metaphor for real talents that individuals have, although I learned differently upon studying the story. Some people are blessed with multiple skills, and others have only basic skills and understanding. Considering the fact that the talents in the story were heavy, it gives a new viewpoint about what it means to carry the responsibility of our own talents. For the sake of the story, though, the "talents" and the servants' abilities are separated.

Let's label everything in the parable! The master is God, of course. The servants are equal to followers of God, whether in the Old Covenant or New Covenant. "Talents" represent anything that God gives for us to have dominion or responsibility over. The doubled amounts of talents are equal to creating fruit for the kingdom, which in the mindset of a New Covenant believer means to reach more souls for Christ, as well as grow in our own relationship with God. We can give each servants' "own abilities" descriptions as follows: the servant with five talents knows how to hook a wagon to two horses and can speak three languages, allowing him to transport his currency further and do business with more people of different languages; the servant with two talents knows how to properly ride a mule and can speak two languages; and the servant with one talent only knows how to carry the talent of gold or silver and can only speak one language.

According to the abilities that each servant had, they

performed a number of actions in order to produce fruit. I relate this story to WISDOM because it is wise to fear the Lord by always giving him glory in everything we do, as we relate back to Proverbs 1:7; IT IS WISE TO DO AS THE LORD WOULD HAVE DONE AND NOT WHAT OUR OWN WILLS DICTATE. In James 1:5 and 3:17, he outlines the fact that wisdom comes FROM God. "If any of you lack wisdom, let him ask of God, that giveth to all men liberally, and upbraideth not; and it shall be given him." "But the wisdom that is from above is first pure, then peaceable, gentle, and easy to be intreated, full of mercy and good fruits, without partiality, and without hypocrisy."

The wisdom that comes from God's will is MEANT to produce fruit of MULTIPLICATION of his kingdom! We can see this character trait in the first two servants. The servants were not told to go out and multiply the money. They just knew that this was the reason why they were given responsibility over it! They were also not told how long the master would be away; if the master had stayed away longer, those who were multiplying his kingdom would have multiplied it FURTHER! Those who were faithful to their responsibility were interested in growing their own capabilities to deal with more talents, and they were not slothful in their work. Of course, in the New Covenant, Jesus did the work on the cross and does the work inside us so that we become more like him. In this case, though, our "work" is our openness to let the Spirit move in us and lead us.

So now, we find in Matthew 25:24-25 that the third servant was well aware that the master expected multiplication of the one talent, but he was afraid. He didn't specify why he was afraid; perhaps he was afraid of failure, therefore, he probably felt safer not moving and losing the talent in the first place. A modern example of this could be if an alcoholic becomes a Christian but doesn't want to acknowledge the fact that he/she is an alcoholic so that there's no responsibility to need to change. They'd say, "God loves me the way I am! I don't have problems, and I don't have to change!"

In verse 26, the master identified this servant as "wicked" and "slothful." "Wickedness" means to willfully go against, and "slothful" tells us how this servant was wicked, in that he followed his own will and desired to make things "easier" for himself. Nobody is slothful for anyone else's sake besides one's self. Let's attach the description of his possible abilities to the scenario of being wicked and lazy. If his only special ability was to pick up the bagged talent, that would mean that he would have had to carry this 75-pound bag from town to town, house to house, estate to estate, and marketplace to marketplace. If he had doubled the money in trades, he would have had to carry two 75-pound bags back to his master's estate. Either that, or he would have had to make multiple trips with a little money at a time. This was obviously not in this particular servant's job description...but it should have been! One's lack of ability does not excuse his duty, and when God expects his children to do something, he will give us the power to do it, no matter how hard it seems!

Another thing to realize in the depiction of this story is that the servants had more to worry about than multiplying the master's money. They also had to worry about finding food and surviving. Logically, if the first two servants made it their purpose in life to do the will of their master in multiplying his kingdom, that means that they had no time to go out and earn food. So, this means that they survived off of the very talents of money that were given to them, and they still managed to produce double the amount they had! Since the third servant buried his talent, that means that he was not surviving off of the master's money. He went out into the world to earn food in his own ways, making dealings with the people of the world, and not living in any way that showed he was the servant of his master who had gone on a long journey. He would have had to be a servant to others in order to survive. Compare this characteristic to a New Covenant believer; this would mean that such a person does not care about being fruitful by reaching souls for Jesus, AND he/she does not care about growing in relationship or being led by the Holy Spirit! This whole moral is yet another wonderful description we can gather from Jesus' parables, that those who decide to serve two masters or be lukewarm are those who serve wickedness and do not care about multiplying God's kingdom.

Ephesians 5:15-21: "See then that ye walk circumspectly, not as fools, but as wise, redeeming the time, because the days are evil. Wherefore be ye not unwise, but understanding what the will of the Lord is. And be not drunk with wine, wherein is excess; but be filled with the Spirit; speaking to yourselves in psalms and hymns and spiritual songs, singing and making melody in your heart to the Lord; giving thanks always for all things unto God and the Father in the name of our Lord Jesus Christ; submitting yourselves one to another in the fear of God."

# CHAPTER THIRTY-FIVE: SELF-AWARE

"Every day we are to live out being who God calls us to be. We must constantly grow in understanding of who we ARE. First and foremost, we are who GOD SAYS we are. His truth in this matter does not need our understanding in order for it to be reality, but our understanding in our identity is needed in order for us to accept the reality he says is true. So, RENEW your mind in Christ daily and be open to change feelings of complacency, that is, being too comfortable in your identity of which you are currently aware. It's important to understand what and who you are because without this knowledge, you won't know what you are supposed to let God change in you."

God's grace is perfect in Christ. There is no amount of work we can do to earn heaven. We simply need to believe in Christ and surrender our lives to him. A big obstacle in the way of surrendering our lives daily to Christ is our own wills which can be found in sinful identity. As we have covered, the reason why we must renew our minds is to adhere to the truth that is in Christ; after the truth in Christ teaches us to die to our own wills, we can expect our lives to change from the inside out over time, if not instantly. I know for myself that my biggest problem was not knowing myself. It got in the way of everything that I did. Without a purpose in life, I was ready to die at any moment; I hardly tried in life. God had grace on me and allowed me to learn everything I could about who I am as a person, my habits, my strengths, the desires of my heart, my weaknesses, etc. Then God led me to the Umbrella-Belief Meeting through a serious of events. Through that church family, he led me to truth and my identity in Christ. Once I was able to learn who I actually was in Christ, despite what I thought my identity was beforehand, I was able to learn what it was that I needed to fully surrender to him. Consider that what you'd think you're supposed to surrender to God is like a big mole on your back that you can't reach, see, or feel because it's numb and growing into cancer. It helps you a lot to finally learn about that mole, in that you can finally choose to go to a doctor (or the Healer) to have it removed. BUT once becoming self-aware in the identity of Christ instead of just knowing who you were before Christ, it's like the Healer literally exchanges the skin on your whole body to that of perfection. In this case, I never should have needed to learn about who I was before Christ if becoming self-aware in who God says that I am made me completely new, but God used my discovery of who I was beforehand to lead me to a point of accepting my real identity in him!

This may seem like a strange Word from God for some of us, but despite our need to learn who we are before accepting Christ, God is basically saying, "Come as you are. Know me so that I can remake you into my identity!" Becoming self-aware of who you were in the past is nice, but becoming self-aware in who God says you are is the goal!

# CHAPTER THIRTY-SIX: WORDS

Becoming SELF-AWARE is heavily dependent upon truth. In such, the identity that we take on is heavily dependent on the words we speak over our lives. There is life and death in the power of words. When you declare falsehoods into your life, you are opening yourself up to being used by the enemy. Always speak truth over your lives out loud. Denounce all lies with which you've come into agreement. The concept of the "Law of Attraction" may have been influenced by this principal, but speaking out truth about yourself or your future is righteous, SPECIFICALLY when we are speaking GOD'S TRUTHS about ourselves. "You are what you eat," is better understood as, "You are what you absorb." When you speak, you absorb those words back into you. Be careful what you say. "Speak what is true."

Matthew 12:36: "But I say unto you, That every idle word that men shall speak, they shall give account thereof in the day of judgement."

# CHAPTER THIRTY-SEVEN: OVERCOME

Jesus highlights the importance of overcoming the world until the very end. Revelation 3:21: "To him that overcometh will I grant to sit with me in my throne, even as I also overcame, and am set down with my Father in his throne." Jesus overcame with faith, believing his Father's words continuously, up to the very end of his life. We are to do the same and never deny Christ, who is our admission into knowing the Holy Spirit. Overcoming the world is a life of continuously choosing the Holy Spirit. It isn't a once-and-done choice. 1 John 5:4: "For whatsoever is born of God overcometh the world: and this is the victory that overcometh the world, even our faith."

# CHAPTER THIRTY-EIGHT: PARADIGM

"Paradigm" means, "a typical pattern or example of something; a model." [18] I asked God, "What is his paradigm towards us as his creation? What is the purpose for our existence?" I understand that Christ is the model we are supposed to emulate, but God answered me further about it through the song "How He Loves" with the words, "we are his portion and He is our prize." That reminded me about the Levites in how they were to receive their portion from the other tribes of Israel in order to gain sustenance but also that God is "their portion." Inversely, God has purchased all things with the blood of Christ. He will inherit all nations (Psalm 82:8), and we are all that he'll take with him once everything on earth ends. So, he is letting life carry on, waiting for all people to be born of whom he knows would choose Christ. He's waiting for the harvest of those souls because he doesn't want any person left behind! 1 Corinthians 13:13 says, "And now abideth faith, hope, and charity, these three; but the greatest of these is charity." Charity is a type of love that is given. Faith creates hope. The reason why love is the greatest is because that's what all of existence is for. The law of God which existed before, during, and after the Old and New

Covenants is summed up into two fundamentals: love God; and love people. Because God is just and lawful, he also loves himself. It is for his name's sake that he created mankind as a companion of whom to love and would love him back, who would praise him for all eternity. It's no coincidence that God teaches us/gives us faith and hope so that we can <u>become HIS LOVE</u>, and that faith, hope, and love are the only things that will not vanish away (as paralleled in 1 Corinthians 13:8: "Charity never faileth: but whether there be prophecies, they shall fail; whether there be tongues, they shall cease; whether there be knowledge, it shall vanish away).

# CHAPTER THIRTY-NINE: FURNACE OF AFFLICTION

Isaiah 48:9-11 says, "For my name's sake will I defer mine anger, and <u>for my praise</u> will I refrain for thee, that I cut thee not off. Behold, I have refined thee, but not with silver; I have chosen thee in the furnace of affliction."

When metals are refined, including the process that was implemented during Bible times, silver was used in the process as a tool towards purification. In relation to refining his people (those who would choose God), "silver" would be interpreted as God simply taking the impurities out by his own devices and power with us not having any choices in the process. But God doesn't choose this; he chooses us in "the furnace of affliction."

So, what is this affliction? It is our environment of a sinful world. Sin in the world is the only thing that truly AFFLICTS ANYTHING outside of God's righteous judgements. The furnace relates to his justice. Those who go through the affliction of sin around them in their lives but still choose Christ to be saved, they will have gone through God's purification process as a new creature, where those who choose to remain impure by not knowing the Holy Spirit will be wasted. This all has to do with the

Fear of the Lord (Word #30). The fear of the Lord has many descriptions in proverbs, but one verse that relates to Proverbs 1:7 is Job 28:28. "And unto man he said, Behold, the fear of the Lord, that is wisdom; and to depart from evil is understanding." I highlight Wisdom because it reveals the state of being that Adam and Eve had before the fall, or more like the lack thereof. Wisdom is knowledge and the ability to use it correctly. It leads to glorifying God to the fullest. Without knowledge, Adam and Eve couldn't have the fear of the Lord with which to choose to glorify God fully, even though they were made perfect. They were simply dwelling in the garden, enjoying creation. I believe this is why God left the tree of the knowledge of good and evil out in the open instead of having it guarded by angels to not be initially touched. Isaiah 46:9-11: "Remember the former things of old: for I am God, and there is none else; I am God, and there is none like me, declaring the end from the beginning, and from ancient times the things that are not yet done, saying, My counsel shall stand, and I will do all my pleasure: calling a ravenous bird from the east, the man that executeth my counsel from a far country: yea, I have spoken it, I will also bring it to pass: I have purposed it, I will also do it."

Imagine if the tree of the knowledge of good and evil was just a different tree. Imagine if it was the "tree of beautiful thorns" and that the only reason why God made it was because it looked pretty but not to eat because it was dangerous. When God would have commanded Adam and Eve to not eat of the tree because it would kill them, Satan would have tempted them into sin, and they would be worthy of death without having knowledge to know how to please God afterwards. In fact, they would have been filled with the knowledge that Satan gave them, which is to not believe God's words that the tree would kill them.

Humanity would have been a lost cause! Therefore, the tree of the knowledge of good and evil is purposed towards creating the perfect human, refined and made new, one who has the capacity to glorify God forever after having received the Holy Spirit through Jesus Christ.

Understand that although God does not create sin, he knew that sin entering into the world could be used as a tool to cause the creation of a better human once he provided the means of destroying sin for good. God could not create humans with the knowledge of good and evil AND make them perfect at the same time because that would make us equal to him, and that would go against his law of loving himself and of being magnified over all things. Humans needed to attain the knowledge of good and evil after the fact in order to attain the opportunity of true free will, which we use to become perfected creations through Christ. Better humans, in this case, are those who were not created equal with God, attained the knowledge of good and evil to become like God, having free will, and yet still choose God over ourselves. It's amazing when you realize this truth, that ALL the time on earth and ALL things made on earth have been purposed as one BIG creation process towards a finished product: worthy believers who choose him forever.

# CHAPTER FOURTY: CHILD OF GOD

Matthew 19:14: "But Jesus said, Suffer little children, and forbid them not, to come unto me: for <u>of such is</u> the kingdom of heaven." We are to be like children; in which way should we be like children? Galatians 3:26 says, "For ye are all the children of God <u>by faith</u> in Christ Jesus." We need to have faith in Christ like children. What does that look like? When a child grows up, he/she is a blank slate. When they are told something, they automatically believe it without questioning. Their faith is unwavering because that is all they know. Children are also joyful and loving. Everything that a child is can show how man's innocence was before the fall. So will we become when we are transformed by the Holy Spirit after having sacrificed the old man by being born again in Christ.

# CHAPTER FOURTY-ONE: CONCLUSION – IDENTITY

If one could not have noticed already, ALL of these words of the day play a part or make up our identity as believers in Christ. In fact, there are actually MORE words that describe our identity as believers in Christ which were not covered in this book! God is so vast, so it only makes sense that this book about your identity is not his last words. We can't have ANY identity without Christ. So, who does God want us to be? Let's review and sum up all of the Words of the Day as they relate to our identity.

We are disciples, friends, and prophets who are made righteous through having faith and relationship in Jesus Christ. God has chosen us to BE HOLY vessels, in which we are restored to original glory upon receiving his inhabitance and living in his Spirit. We are holy warriors who defend the truth of Christ's salvation by LIVING it out in all authority, with 100% devotion and surrender which is given towards the purpose and plan of being those with freedom, boldness, joy, faith, praise, and patience to overcome ALL adversities, even if it means giving up our lives so that we are never forced by the world to deny devotion to the Holy Spirit that we attain through Christ.

ALL of this exists to give God GLORY! All of life exists and is purposed towards molding and growing believers who choose him and love him forever.

— Amen

# CHAPTER FOURTY-TWO: COMPLETE AFFIRMATIONS LIST

The definition of "affirmation" is, "something declared to be true; a positive statement or judgement." [20] When God taught me about speaking affirmations over my life whilst writing this book, it couldn't have been more beneficial to my spiritual walk than anything else. Writing a list of God's truths in my life forced me to see how my heart posture was operating. My list started small, then it grew into at least twenty statements. I realized that my statements were hardly positive at all. The demonic whispers from the world had permeated my understanding over the years, and I was left with a nihilistic view of my identity and reality, knowing the truth that God is above all and deserving of my praise, but that I was worthless. The list consisted of entries like, "My will is not my idol. There is nothing good in my flesh, and I will not let it be my idol. My flesh is in league with the devil, and I will live in the Spirit of God instead of the flesh." These statements are basically true, but they are missing other truths that generate good fruit in my spiritual walk. The way that I stated them was basically a declaration of the negative beliefs about myself. So, I was causing the opposite of what was supposed to be happening. I was experiencing demonic dreams of torment and pain. My condition of tinnitus that I've had literally all my life was starting to flare up like nails on a chalkboard! (The ringing in my head became so loud that I was able to identify the frequencies when I looked them up online using a free frequency generator. The two loudest frequencies I hear 24/7, even in my dreams, are 8055 Hz and 430 Hz.) As I had begun to learn more about my identity in Christ, denouncing all lies from my life and accepting all of God's truths, the tinnitus lessened so much that I can barely notice the sounds most of the time. When I live in peace through Christ, freedom in my spirit and my body follows!

If this is your first time reading this book, you should treat this section as a personal spiritual experiment. Before reading the list below, take some time to write down a list of your own about what you believe concerning your identity and reality. Compare your list to mine, and see where you stand spiritually. This isn't the section where I am telling you that I'm better than you! The more I worked on my list and its wording, the more I fashioned the list to different Bible verses that tell us who we are in Christ. I used to have to read this affirmation list daily, but when I finally engrained truth into my heart, I found myself needing to read this list less and less because I was simply living out the truth. I pray the same results for you!

- These affirmations are declarations of truth, not magic spells that make my day better. I will repeat them for my benefit of building belief and faith through the love of Jesus Christ and relationship with God's Holy Spirit. It is God who works the growth in my heart, not my own works. With meekness, I receive his gift of change; with prayer, I diligently seek relationship with God. A measure of faith saves me; replacing my desires with God's desires makes me full of faith. (Romans 12:3; Matthew 5:5; 1 Thessalonians 5:17; Isaiah 58:13-14; Hebrews 11:6)

- I am a child of God! (John 1:12)
- I am CHOSEN! I am a royal priest! I am holy and special because of Christ! (1 Peter 2:9)
- God says I am full of faith because I diligently seek relationship with him! (Hebrews 11:6)
- God has wiped self-pity and fear from my heart and given me a spirit of power, love, and of sound mind! This is a result of the gift of the Holy Spirit. (2 Timothy 1:7)
- Relationship with God teaches me not to have a complaining spirit; trying of my faith in trials and temptations builds my patience because I have joy in the Lord and only want God to receive all the glory! (James 1:2-4)
- I do not condemn myself anymore because Christ was not sent to condemn but to save the world through him; I am made righteous through Christ and choose to live holy through him forever! (John 3:17-18)
- I will trust in the Lord with all my heart and lean not on my own understanding. I will not submit to my emotions, feelings, impulses of the flesh, or temptations of sin thereof because I will acknowledge God in all my ways! He will direct me! (Proverbs 3:5-6)
- I have been purchased by the blood of Christ; my body, mind, and spirit belong to God! I am his beautiful, elaborate TEMPLE, and I am more

beautiful than any temple that has ever existed! (1 Corinthians 6:19-20; 1 Kings chapters 5-7; search online for a 3D rendition of Solomon's temple![20])

- I am precious in the sight of the Lord! (Psalms 116:15)
- I continuously choose to have faith in Christ, now and forever! I choose to have Christ's faith! (Philippians 3:8-11)
- My faith is manifested through the promises fulfilled by the finished work of the cross, which is God's love for us, in that when I confess Christ, I am saved. (Romans 10:9-10)
- I will not live in order to please men, but everything I do, I will perform it as service to God! I will not live in order to please myself. Lord, teach me how to please you in everything I do. (Ephesians 6:6-7)
- I renounce the lusts of the flesh of food and sexual pleasures, and I put on the full armor of God, walking in the ways of the Spirit! (Romans 8; Galatians 5; Ephesians 6)
- Every thought I have will be held captive into the obedience of Christ; I renounce coarse language, crude and sexual thoughts, and negative mindsets that glorify my own will! (2 Corinthians 10:3-6)
- I have forgiven my past as God has forgiven my past! I have forgiven those who have hurt me just as God has forgiven me! And I pray that if I have not forgiven someone, that the Holy Spirit will make it known to me so that I may forgive. I live through God's correction. (Matthew 18:35; Hebrews 12:10-11)
- I am FREE from affliction and evil done towards me! I am not a victim! (Jeremiah 15:11)

- Jesus is Master over my health! (Isaiah 53:5-6)
- There is no evil in my spirit anymore, only righteousness through Christ! (Romans 8:10)
- My body is FREE from the rule of sin because Christ has been placed above all principalities, powers, might, and dominion. When I live life in his Spirit, I honor God in my body! (Ephesians 1; Romans 8:3-4; 2 Corinthians 4:7-10)
- I am not afraid of the cares of the world! (Psalms 23:4; Luke 12:24-26)
- God provides for me! (Matthew 6:31-33; Philippians 4:19)
- I will not live as one who is self-centered, caring about my own life selfishly, but in every up and down in my life, I will remember that it is all geared towards excelling the kingdom of God here on earth. I have peace in Christ! (2 Corinthians 4:17-18)
- I am powerless to overcome adversities WITHOUT Christ! (John 15:4-5)
- I have his love in me and diligently seek God to BE his love! (Luke 10:27-37)
- My identity is not what I feel in my emotions or circumstances; it is what God says it is! (Romans 8:28)

I encourage you to read this list periodically, every time you need to remember your identity in Christ. Never forget who he says you are! The more you denounce lies and accept truth that is in God's Word, the more your life will change! Meditate on Christ daily. Remember, there's nothing magic about this list; it's simply all about learning how to know God the Father and his Son Jesus Christ!

# CHAPTER FOURTY-THREE: SERMON ABOUT FAITH

What is faith?

Hebrews 11:1: "Now faith is the substance of things hoped for, the evidence of things not seen."

Hebrews 11:6: "But without faith it is impossible to please him: for he that cometh to God must believe that he is, and that he is a rewarder of them that diligently seek him."

These two verses alone touch on four things:

1. Faith IS belief.

2. This belief retains itself as "evidence" on a personal level that is REAL and able to have "substance" in a person's life. (ex. your experience of a miracle, God talking to you, etc.)

3. It is impossible to please God without faith (belief) IN HIM, and specifically in Jesus Christ as will be mentioned in other verses.

4. The ACTION of belief is described as "diligently seeking" God.

Romans 12:3 briefly touches on the fact that God provides "a measure of faith" to believers. When we compare this fact with the above-mentioned verses in

Hebrews, we have to ask, "What is it that God provides when faith is synonymously linked to our belief?" God answered me today...and that's it. God ANSWERED! He gives "a measure of faith" to believers BY giving answers and experiences from which we derive hope in God's promises. You can't have hope without faith because faith is the "substance" of hope. God supplies WHY we have faith.

There are a few more examples of faith I'd like to touch on. First, asking this: "Who has perfect faith?" God is the only one who has perfect faith. He demonstrates this many times, the first demonstration of which we know is creation itself. GOD SPOKE, and because of his power of faith, he makes things become real. This power of faith is manifested to us in the gifts of the Holy Spirit, to which we have authority to use within God's will. He grants this to us because he lives in us and loves us. He wants to provide this POWER in us like a "shield of faith" protects us in battle. It protects us from the lies of the enemy, but a "shield" in battle can also be used to "slap" down an opponent, in this case, against the unbelief of a person for which we might pray to become healed or receive some other sort of miracle.

There are many references to the gifts of the Holy Spirit, the most specific list found in 1 Corinthians 12:8-10. The 9 gifts are a Word of Wisdom, Word of Knowledge, Faith, Gifts of Healings, Miracles, Prophecy, Discerning spirits, Tongues, and Interpretations of Tongues. The teachings of Dr. Lester Sumrall say that ALL these gifts of the Spirit are manifested THROUGH FAITH (belief) and PURPOSED in God's love. If you don't believe the gifts will happen (belief in God's power), they won't work. If you're performing the gifts outside of God's love (like witchcraft abuses the powers in God's creation), the gifts won't work.

It's important to note the difference between faith as BELIEF and faith as POWER. Even looking at the gifts of the Holy Spirit as a whole, the faith which is belief is needed to make all the gifts work, including faith as a power to manifest miracles.

So, we have found these things to be synonymous with each other in scripture: faith; belief; substance as evidence of the unseen; God's words spoken to us directly or through scripture.

I'd like to focus on his words and character. God has perfect love; therefore, God IS love. Christ has perfect faith; therefore, he IS faith. (God just told me to specifically word that sentence about Christ for a very important reason!) But how are these things brought about? Love manifests in ACTIONS found in 1 Corinthians chapter 13. Faith manifests through WORDS, as many verses mention like Romans 10:17. "So then faith cometh by hearing, and hearing by the word of God." So, faith comes from the Words of God! The Words of God can be directly from him to you, from scripture, or from any way God decides to communicate. This relates to Romans 12:3 where God gives us "a measure of faith" by speaking to us in an experience. God is always the one who takes the first step, just like it mentions in 1 John 4:19. "We love him, because he loved us first."

I'm going to deviate into a supportive set of ideas that build towards new understandings about faith. I once asked God to give me a revelation of his truth; I started a list of questions that weren't getting answered...until I had enough questions. I asked, "What is the nature of the universe in relation to how You started it?" "How can there be Father and Son who are of the same Spirit?" "How is Christ 'begotten' [when 'begotten' usually implies that someone or something was created within a genealogy] if he was not 'created' and was always with the Father?"

The Holy Spirit started to give me understanding and reminded me of Jesus visiting the disciples after his resurrection. Jesus had a glorified body, a spiritual body. Then I thought about how people see spirits all the time on earth and how we, as spirits, occupy bodies. Biblically, King Saul had seen Samuel's spirit in person, as it was supposed. Seeing spirits cannot be denied. These spiritual instances happening in the physical world must mean that the physical world is SPIRITUAL AS WELL, just pieced together differently. How else could these realms co-exist? It is the visible and the invisible of the same realm!

(I have also been made aware of certain verses that suggest that demons being trapped inside the physical portion of this realm, being disconnected from God's Spirit, and not being able to travel through the limitlessness of the invisible spiritual world like they were able in the Old Testament times…is like hell on earth to them. 2 Peter 2:4: "For if God spared not the angels that sinned, but cast them down to hell, and delivered them into chains of darkness, to be reserved unto judgement;" Jude 1:6: "And the angels which kept not their first estate, but left their own habitation, he hath reserved in everlasting chains under darkness unto the judgement of the great day." 1 John 1:5: "This then is the message which we have heard of him, and declare unto you, that God is light, and in him is no darkness at all." It is clear to me that since the demons are disconnected from God's light (where disconnection from God is equal to spiritual death), they are forever trapped in darkness and limited in the physical world, especially after they were cast out of heavenly places, as depicted in Revelation 12:9, which says they were cast out into the earth! The limited boundaries makes earth a perfect holding place before the final judgement!)

The science and math started to spiral through my head. I remembered scientific studies I read in my youth about how scientists found that atoms are divisible down to many sublevels; the only thing that stops scientists from dividing atoms further is the lack of technology. The point of bringing this up is that, mathematically speaking, if anything retains a numeric value that can be divided, it can technically be divided infinitely! So, just as the nothingness of space is infinitely wide, so it is that matter itself is infinitely capable of division! Because of this and the fact that spiritual things have happened on this physical plane, I argue that created matter is spiritual as well. It's as if the makeup of physical matter is compressed, dense spiritual energy. Although, in the matter of sharing facts, I share this viewpoint as just a theory right now because I have no way of scientifically proving it... I'm not a physicist! I would have coined this as "The Theory of Spiritual Relativity," but that title has unfortunately already been taken.

Anyway, one day after that revelation, I was watching a sermon online. The preacher finished a thought and said, "Jesus knew the words to say. He IS the WORD!" Just then, my eyes were opened and I could see the answers to my other questions revealed! There are verses and references in the makeup of the Hebrew language that suggest that God's words are living and breathing. Jesus himself says in John 6:63, "The words I speak to you, they are spirit, and they are life." John 1:1-3 says, "In the beginning was the Word, and the Word was with God, and the Word was God. The same was in the beginning with God. All things were made by him [the Word]; and without him was not any thing made that was made." John 1:14 describes who the Word is. "And the Word was made flesh, and dwelt among us, (and we beheld his glory, the glory as the only begotten of the Father,) full of grace and truth." John 1:18: "No man hath seen God at any time; the only begotten Son, which is in the bosom of the Father, he [the Son] hath declared him."

**These verses in John are saying that Christ IS the ACTUAL WORDS that were BEGOTTEN from the BOSOM of God's Spirit when God CREATED EVERYTHING!**

**"LET THERE BE LIGHT." These words of God and all the rest of the words in Genesis chapter 1 (and everywhere else) ARE CHRIST!**

**This is how the Father and Son are of one Spirit! Picture, if you will, the Father and Son being a part of the same spiritual "body" just as the church will be married to his Holy Spirit, described in the book of Revelation. God is so Perfect and Sovereign that ANYTHING that comes OUT of God's Spirit IS LIFE and ALIVE.**

God is an invisible Spirit with no body. He doesn't pee or poop, sweat or cry. He has no semen...The ONLY things that CAN come OUT of God's Spirit are his WORDS and his breath. So, when God spoke, Christ came out (never as a created being, as the word "begotten" can be understood, because God could always speak, so Christ WAS and IS always God's words) and pulled together all physical things into existence. Going back to the fact that God doesn't have semen, when he impregnated Mary, it only makes sense that the only thing that comes OUT of his Spirit are his Words...and Christ was the result after God spoke into her womb. This whole topic about the answer to my questions being that Christ IS GOD'S WORDS may seem to be off topic with the subject of faith...But it's NOT! We can now attribute the definitions of "faith" DIRECTLY to Christ's character! Because faith comes from the **Words of God**. Faith comes from Christ. Christ IS faith. It only makes sense that we cannot please God without faith; we cannot please God without believing in Christ, without believing God's Words. It is even said about Abraham in Genesis 15:6, "And he believed in the LORD; and he counted it to him for righteousness." Believing in God's words to be saved has ALWAYS been a thing!

In the above paragraph, I mentioned that God's "breath" also comes out of him. Although this is a continued deviation away from this current deviation about Christ being THE WORDS of God, it's important not to leave out the Holy Spirit in the full explanation. To be frank, God the Father and Jesus Christ ARE the Holy Spirit together, described as "the Comforter" in John 14:23-26, but this book has nothing to do with challenging the Trinity doctrine. I have no clue if the fact that the Father and Son are one Spirit makes them a "third person" together or not, as if the Spirit is a fusion of the Father and Son who retains all the identifying qualities of each, but as one. For all we know, that could be the case. It's just another thing we can be happy to ask God in heaven someday! I'd like to highlight John 20:22, quoting 21-23: "Then said Jesus to them again, Peace be unto you: as my Father hath sent me, even so send I you. And when he had said this, he breathed on them, and saith unto them, Receive ye the Holy Ghost: Whose soever sins ye remit, they are remitted unto them; and whose soever sins ye retain, they are retained." The following is an excerpt which explains the transliteration of the phrase, "he breathed on them," which is "emphysao," meaning, "to blow or breathe upon:"

"The Greek word here used is employed nowhere else in the New Testament, but is the very one used by the

Septuagint translators of Gen 2:7: 'And the Lord God formed man of the dust of the ground, and *breathed* into his nostrils the breath of life; and man became a living soul.' There, man's original creation was completed by this act of God; who, then, can fail to see that here in John 20, on the day of the Saviour's resurrection, the *new creation* had begun, begun by the Head of the new creation, the last Adam acting as 'a quickening spirit' (1Cr 15:45)!" (Arthur W. Pink, *Exposition of the Gospel of John*, p. 1100).

I have come to understand, then, that the Holy Spirit is the "spiritual essence" of who God is and does not just come out of God, but it is what is "above all, and through all, and in you all." (Ephesians 4:6) Furthermore, when we dive deeper into the transliteration meaning of John 3:8, for example, we see that the same Greek word "pneuma" is used for the phrase "the wind" as well as for "Spirit." [21] "THE WIND bloweth where it listeth, and thou hearest the sound thereof, but canst not tell whence it cometh, and whither it goeth: so is every one that is born of the SPIRIT." So, "Wind" is the descriptive earthly name of the spiritual essence or breath that comes out of God and gives life, the Holy Spirit. Even so, John 6:63 says as well, "The words I speak to you, they are spirit [pneuma], and they are life."

I'd like to go back to an example of faith that points to an interesting set of ideas and understandings. This is the story of the "sore vexed" child and how the disciples could not heal him, but Jesus did. (Found in Matthew 17:14-21) The disciples asked him why they couldn't cast the demon out. (vs 20-21) "And Jesus said unto them, Because of your unbelief: for verily I say unto you, If ye have faith as a grain of mustard seed, ye shall say unto this mountain, Remove hence to yonder place; and it shall remove; and nothing shall be impossible unto you. Howbeit this kind [of faith that moves mountains] goeth not out but by prayer and fasting." Most people think that "kind" in this verse is referring to the demon that was in the child. When I look at the transliterations of Matthew 17:21 and Mark 9:29, "kind" in the Strongs for both verses is "genos, c1085," which means "kindred, offspring, family, stock, tribe, nation, or those of the same nature." So, it looks like they are right when they say that "kind" refers to the demon, but the reason why I put "of faith that moves mountains" in brackets (equating to "kind") is because of the context of the sentences. Why would Jesus say that nothing would be impossible to the disciples but then right away explain a situation where it'd be impossible to cast out the demon without prayer and fasting. If he is saying, "It is because of your unbelief that you are not able to cast the demon out," and then he explains that they can move mountains with the smallest of faith, it makes sense that the two feats are equal, rather it doesn't matter what kind of feat it is. The faith that it takes to move mountains is the same faith that it takes to cast the demon out.

I like how Jesus linked the definitions of belief and faith in verse 20, but I have to say that I was confused at first about FASTING. I understood plainly that prayer means communion with God; makes sense if you're supposed to do a miracle like moving a mountain. What does FASTING have anything to do with faith in this context? How does fasting and prayer grow faith? God describes what he expects from those who fast. Read ALL of Isaiah chapter 58! God begins to rebuke how they fast in a way that they cause strife, debate, trying to make their voices "heard on high."(vs 4)

(vs 5) "Is it such a fast that I have chosen? a day for a man to afflict his soul? is it to bow down his head as a bullrush, and to spread sackcloth and ashes under him? wilt thou call this a fast, and an acceptable day to the LORD?" God gets detailed about how he'd like people to perform a communal fasting for him, and verses 13-14 specify this: "If thou turn away thy foot from the sabbath, from doing thy pleasure on my holy day; and call the sabbath a delight, the holy of the LORD, honourable; and shalt honour him, **not doing thine own ways, nor finding thine own pleasure, nor speaking thine own words**: Then shalt thou delight in the LORD..." THIS WHOLE VERSE IS SAYING THAT WE MUST DIE TO OUR WILL AND **REPLACE IT WITH GOD'S WILL** in order to build faith that moves mountains, replacing our faith with his faith! (I covered Isaiah 58 in a similar fashion for Word #31.) Just as fasting is used to remove something in our lives so that we can replace it with communion with God, the purpose of fasting and prayer to enhance our faith in doing things like "moving mountains" is to replace our desires with God's desires. I'm relating this back to when Jesus said, "Howbeit this kind goeth not out but by prayer and fasting." With this being said, and since we can attribute the character of Christ to faith directly, we can see that Christ lived out his whole time on earth doing NOTHING BUT BEING the WILL of his Father. We should be the same and diligently seek the Father because THAT is the ACTION of faith, and John 17:3 is the purpose and the prize!

"And this is life eternal, that they might know thee the only true God, and Jesus Christ, whom thou hast sent."

# CHAPTER FOURTY-FOUR:
# UNDERSTANDING DELIVERANCE
# AFTER THE FAST

Like I had mentioned previously in the introduction, the Fast was quite an invigorating period in our lives! So many of us at the Umbrella-Belief Meeting had become changed and renewed in many different ways. 2020 was full of obstacles that seemed to restrict the rest of the world, but we flourished in our small groups. God had told us at the beginning of that year that we were going to split up into multiple locations, and the Covid restrictions brought gatherings down to ten people per visit anyway, so it happened just like that. We had seven available meetings all throughout the week in different locations plus one meeting on Sunday afternoons which were devoted to asking God questions concerning deliverance from demons, deliverance studies, et cetera. It was uncharted territory for us all, so Linda had inquired of some experienced minds to help us during our journey to more complete understanding.

Our first guest who joined us via online video conferencing was Steve Koenig of Being Changed Ministry Inc. If you go to the ministry website,[22] you'll find a lot of resources about deliverance, including the Blue and Green deliverance cards. These are tools for guiding people to learn how to break spiritual ties to demonic influences. They are based on referring to the guidance of the Holy Spirit in prayer to reveal things in the "client's" past of which were traumatic events, or mindsets that were based off lies. As these things were revealed, they'd go through the cards to do the process of speaking out against and releasing the traumas or lies. I discovered in my own interpretation that this process of deliverance had MUCH to do with "renewal of the mind," as the Apostles had referenced many times in the New Testament.

So, I was diving deep into this! I wanted to be on the front lines of deliverance as we were learning this process. We started to set up "appointments" where "clients" could go through the card system. (A "client" in this subject is not one who pays for a service, but it is a term that's used to highlight the individual going through deliverance.) I was a consistent deliverance partner with Linda's husband, John, from spring until much of the summer, walking different men through the cards while Linda and other deliverance volunteers helped counsel the women. So, part of this objective I took on was happening during the Fast, while God was still supplying me with the 40 Words of the Day, and the other part took place after that fateful Easter Sunday when we stood outside our houses, speaking out the declarative promises we were making to God as a community. When John and I brought clients through the cards, I noticed something off about the list of "strongmen and underlings." It was quite short! The list on the cards had some important negative mindsets of which to denounce. This process made sense to me because of this reasoning I've mentioned before: God is truth; therefore, all things that oppose God derive from lies. This includes demons! So, if there is a specific "spirit of condemnation," for example, that spirit would be connected to the false mindset of condemnation. The lie is what any demonic influence stands upon! (To be clear, the false mindsets alone are just as dangerous to a person's spiritual walk as it would be if a demonic influence were connected to the mindsets. Lies keep you from walking closer in understanding with God, and they limit the freedom you possess inside your mind. So, these mindsets must be addressed and denounced whether there's demonic influence or not.) And here we were, having the clients go through a miniscule list that had important items to address but didn't even include "pride!" This is what influenced me to research and collect as many, if not all of the genres of negative mindsets and possible demon names which could be attributed to the mindsets. You will find this list in the next couple of chapters.

My involvement in the Being Changed Ministry type of deliverance sessions would begin to become scarce at some point. This mainly occurred because of scheduling issues at first, and then things about the way we did deliverance sessions started to change once we received counsel from a particular deliverance ministry that's based out in California. For the purpose of respecting their ministry within text because I don't necessarily agree with their beliefs, I will label them as "BIDM" which stands for "believes-in-deliverance-ministries." If you search on the web for "deliverance from demons," you will most likely find the real ministry on YouTube, performing extreme deliverances on people who manifest demons. I've met Bart and his protégé, Dylan (as I will refer to them here in this text); they are good gentlemen who love God and are passionate about deliverance ministries! Although I tried being their client and experienced some things spiritually that were pretty traumatizing, I'm glad I went through their system to gain understanding. God used their system to take care of at least 20% of my problems, and the rest of the issues were handled in personal communion and meditation with God. (One of my problems was that I was holding onto trinkets from my past that I didn't realize were connected to witchcraft: stones, to be specific. I threw them into a river and personally went through the Blue and Green cards to denounce idolatry. Other problems included the need to denounce several false mindsets about my personal worth.) God used this experience to help me be open to listening to him about my issues. The experiences I had during and after that session with Bart were eye-opening concerning the understanding of how the spirit world works...and it's clear to me that it doesn't work completely the same way that people particularly think it works!

Although I had received a particular understanding about deliverance, the rest of the people in the Umbrella-Belief Meeting had not received the exact same revelations. Upon further searching for truth, Linda had received an impartation from Bart to receive a double portion of what he does in deliverance ministries, according to her story, of which she may tell in the book she's planning on writing. As a result, people have been flocking to her, consistently setting up times to meet and become delivered from demonic influence. It was an inclination that the rest of us at the Umbrella-Belief Meeting had not fully grasped how to do yet. Suffice to say, I won't do it in the same way, but I will not bash her or the ministry if that's what she is called to specifically do and if it's not what I'm supposed to do exactly the same way. We've seen many people get set free from this movement, and I pray that this fruit continues! In the meantime, for myself, I'm focusing on what God is specifically teaching me about Identity, Faith, and Deliverance.

The Holy Spirit has led me into completely different paths concerning ministering to people. As I mentioned before, God is calling me to reach lukewarm Christians, first starting with this book, and then into the leading of acquiring facilities in which pastors will have the ability to start churches. My tithe and offering will be a free rent, as God revealed to me in a vision! Towards the end of 2020, I was also led to join a new church, Grace Nation, under Pastor Gerry Mickle. I had received many prophecies at his ministry, and many of the things that the Holy Spirit had taught me in this book, the Spirit had also been inspiring this pastor to preach. God used Pastor Gerry's sermons as confirmation that the Spirit had truly inspired me to write this book! I've been extremely blessed to experience both church families!

It wasn't easy for me to deal with the changes that were initially happening at the Umbrella-Belief Meeting. Although I had no extremely hard feelings towards the people at the Umbrella-Belief Meeting nor at the BIDM, some differences in doctrine started to arise that really shook my spirit. BIDM has an understanding that Spirit-filled Christians can retain demon possession inside their bodies through invitations made personally or passed down generationally from ancestors. This hypothesis comes from a very well-drawn connection of verses which equate the Old Testament temple structure to how the spiritual structure of human beings is derived. Simply put, they believe that the physical flesh is the same as the Outer Courts of the temple; the mind, thoughts, and emotions are the Inner Courts; and the place where a Christian's spirit and the Holy Spirit reside inside is the same as the Holy of Holies. Logically, they deduce that since the Old Testament

Israelites defiled the Outer Courts of the temple with Pagan worship, sacrifices, and demonic influence on multiple occasions, human flesh can be defiled and indwelled by demons as well, even if the Holy Spirit is in the "Holy of Holies" that is inside Christians at the same time. My spirit couldn't accept that for some reason; there was something very wrong here! I almost felt like believing in this particular doctrine was heresy against the Holy Spirit because I believe that the sacrifice of Christ pays for the authority over the spirit, mind, AND body. Any other "work" that's needed in order to be delivered from evil besides the work of Christ on the cross goes against what is understood as the "simplicity of the gospel." I will provide more details about my take on "possessions versus oppressions of Spirit-filled Christians" in the next chapter.

Furthermore, concerning the doctrines of the BIDM, Bart had proposed during multiple deliverance sessions that I experienced that even he couldn't be too sure if he had expelled the complete number of demons from his own flesh over the decades that he had been doing this ministry. While these doctrines were being adopted into the Umbrella-Belief Meeting and studied for further understanding, I even heard an implication that the "evil that is in the flesh" that Paul the Apostle mentions in Romans chapter 7 could be equivalent to demonic indwelling! I'm so thankful to God for showing me the Nazarene Vow in this book! As I've seen, none of these ministries I've mentioned have ever referenced the Nazarene Vow and how it quite relates to why the sin of the flesh was left in the body of Christians. I believe it has much to do with solving this confusion that we've experienced while trying to understand demonic deliverance better.

There was one point where I had learned of another

Umbrella-Belief Meeting leader's doctrinal viewpoint compared to that of the BIDM. He believes that once a person accepts Christ and receives the Holy Spirit, that person is spiritually sealed and cannot lose the Holy Spirit; if a person truly denies the Holy Spirit, that person wasn't really a Christian to begin with. BUT he believes as I do that demons cannot dwell inside Christian flesh. BIDM believes as I do that a Christian could decide to walk away from the faith and from the Holy Spirit, thereby being able to lose salvation. So, understand how this sounds, and let's see if this makes sense. One believes that a Christian is sealed and safe from demonic indwelling, but doesn't that particular understanding imply that the Christian will NEVER KNOW if he is truly saved until he makes it to heaven? The other side believes that flesh is not necessarily safe from demons, nor can we know if all the demons have left the flesh, despite the Holy Spirit being present inside the Christian. They also believe that a Christian can lose salvation if he chooses to deny Christ. So, if a demon has a big impact on influencing what one believes, doesn't this second premise imply that it's possible that true freedom and salvation can never be achieved? These are both worst-case scenarios of these ideas. Confusion like this is the main reason why I had to step away from constant attendance of the Umbrella-Belief Meeting; I would have been too outspoken about doctrines and butted heads with leadership. That's something I didn't want to do, as I love them like family.

I did recently visit Linda during the time I was rewriting this chapter, though. Upon further questioning, I believe that Linda and I have come to a middle ground concerning the scenarios of opposing viewpoints that I mentioned in the previous paragraph. The biggest difference that we have right now is that although she doesn't want to deny that

Christians can be indwelled by demons (at least, that's my impression), she also believes that inward possession and outward oppression is equally dangerous, and therefore it doesn't matter if we can prove that demons are inside or outside; THEY NEED TO BE HANDLED. While I appreciate that and agree that they must be handled, I differ in view in that it's important to be correct about ALL the truth! It's my impression that any lie that a Christian believes can allow a demon to have a foothold in order to affect a Christian's life somewhere down the road, even concerning the smallest of details. Another big difference Linda and I have is that she has been granted a special grace to perform deliverance ministry as one of her focused responsibilities, while that is not my focused calling at the moment. As I questioned her more about how her ministry was doing, I was encouraged to find out that the way she performs deliverances has evolved passed what Being Changed Inc. and BIDM has systematically performed. Her sessions have become more "organic," as she put it. I discovered that there are many similarities between what God had taught her and what God had taught me over this past year! We both agree that deliverance needs to start with the Holy Spirit before anything. Identity and relationship in Christ fuels freedom (while the other two ministries believe this as well, it didn't seem to be a focal point during debates I had with them, hence why I highlight that Linda seems to organically make that a focus during the deliverances). I like what Evangelist Ted Shuttlesworth Jr. said on one of his broadcasts: "Being led by the Spirit brings deliverance." That hits the nail on the head! Every deliverance is different and requires the leading of the Holy Spirit throughout the whole process. As I have been led in different directions than Linda has been led by the Holy Spirit, I have been comforted in the fact that I don't have to worry about the differences in doctrines somehow being blasphemy. If God is leading her path, following that leading is not blasphemy. God is the best realist EVER, and he's using both of us to reach souls for Christ, despite differences in understanding about that one doctrine. I can't wait to see what kind of fruit her ministry will bear, especially after she writes her book about deliverance!

# CHAPTER FORTY-FIVE: "POSSESSIONS VS OPRESSIONS" OF SPIRIT-FILLED CHRISTIANS

As I mentioned, a minor discrepancy in doctrines popped up after we received advice from the BID Ministries. It's something that seems minor to some people. It can be chocked off as "irrelevant" or put on the list of things that "we'll just have to ask God when we get to heaven." But the debate about whether or not a Spirit-filled Christian is able to have their body possessed by a demon is not something that I was ready to just sit on and blindly accept. I couldn't just leave the stone unturned and not figure it out, either! As I had mentioned in the previous chapter, having the WHOLE truth concerning identity, faith, and deliverance in Christ is important in order to experience full freedom in every aspect of one's walk of life. God had spent the better part of two months to a year while I've been writing this book, teaching me about IDENTITY in Christ and the simplicity of the Gospel, that the only "work" that's required of us to be saved and delivered is to believe in Christ and surrender to him as our Lord. So, I felt like, "Why would God tell others that it takes 'more work?'" This topic did not sit right with my spirit when it felt like "ritual" was taking the place of Christ's work on the cross when it relates to how we are to perform deliverances (at least, that's the first impression I had about the opposing side of this debate when I came to understand their subject).

The truth of the matter is that people were and still continue to get set free from demonic influence under this impartation. Who knows if people are continuing to walk out in freedom? That would take a year alone of documentary research, investigating, and interviewing to deduce! But I would argue that any amount of time entertaining a lie, no matter how small of a lie, is too much of a chance for the devil to gain a foothold to be able to stick around and cause more confusion. The devil is the father of lies; he will put on a show and subtly back off from your life if it means that he can convince you to believe a lie about God. The "show" of which I'm referring (that happened to be a catalyst that caused confusion and division and had caused some people to leave that congregation) is when Spirit-filled Christians were manifesting control of their bodies and words to that of demonic influence during deliverance meetings, flailing around and being used like demonic puppets. In my older, more offended viewpoint where I had thought that entertaining the doctrine of Christians being possessed was much like heresy, I had written much of this chapter before the previous chapter. In my haste, I wrote this as an essay that I would say was not completely inspired by the Holy Spirit. I decided to pause researching the publishing stages of the book and rewrite this whole section on deliverance to better biblically explain why I believe that Christians simply can't have demons dwelling in their bodies if the Holy Spirit is present. A big point to address here is HOW can demons control Christians or bodies in general? Why aren't Spirit-filled Christians manifesting the HOLY SPIRIT instead of demons? While the simplest answer to this question is probably that such Christians weren't really Spirit-filled, many of these people had shown signs of being led by the Holy Spirit during worship, group studies, and in daily life. So, the answer is not specifically that simple, and in all fairness, this needs to be addressed in a non-accusing manner, outlining all the possible scenarios.

The rest of this chapter will include remnants of the essay I mentioned previously but revised and organized according to how the Holy Spirit directed me to fix it. I will include many examples from my life of which I am able to relate to the scriptures I outline. As I will reveal, the "simplest answer" to the above questions I asked, aside from brute strength, is that Christians and non-Christians are able to be moved by demonic forces that use the POWER OF SUGGESTION rather than simply through demonic, indwelling possession.

**JOB'S ACCUSERS** (The original name of the essay)
Job 4:12-21 NASB— Eliphaz the Temanite tells Job words that he received from a spirit. Little does he know that it was Satan filling his ears about how to accuse Job. Let's consider these verses!

"Now a word was brought to me secretly, and my ear received a whisper of it. Amid disquieting thoughts from visions of the night, when deep sleep falls on people, dread came upon me, and trembling, and made all my bones shake. Then a spirit passed by my face; the hair of my flesh stood up. *Something* was standing still, but I could not recognize its appearance; a form *was* before my eyes; there was silence, then I heard a voice: 'Can mankind be righteous before God? Can a man be pure before his Maker? He puts no trust even in His servants; and He accuses His angels of error. How much more those who live in houses of clay, whose foundation is in the dust, who are crushed before the moth! Between morning and evening they are broken in pieces; unregarded, they perish forever. Is their tent-cord not pulled out within them? They die, yet without wisdom.'"

It's important to notice the list of reasons WHY we must understand that this is an evil spirit and not an angel of God. First of all, everywhere else in scripture, whenever a person is approached by an angel, the angel always says some kind of reassuring phrase like, "Fear not." When you are around a spirit, it's an energy-sucking experience! Their very presence around you freezes your body, not just physically but emotionally. This particular spirit that visited Eliphaz did not reassure him or comfort him as one who is an ally, like other angels documented in the Bible would do. Secondly, we can tell by the message this spirit sent that it is not from God. The message is a statement of general truths that are twisted in order to seem just right to a man, but overall, it is a nihilistic message that is stated more out of pity for "the servants" of God who were judged for their sins rather than stated out of the love that comes from God for mankind. Thirdly, in previous chapters of Job, the context of the story shows that the devil had joined other angels in the gathering in the presence of the Lord, and during this time, the devil and God have a conversation about Job and his righteousness. The end result of the conversation was that the devil was reaffirmed in his earthly rights and authority to negatively affect Job's life, simply to prove to God that Job would blaspheme against God. Although the devil had the authority to enter and possess any person during the Old Testament period because authority over the world had transferred from Adam to Satan when Adam and Eve sinned, the devil would not possess Job or others around him so as to not force their decisions or blow his cover of influence in the situation. The devil's pride to prove God wrong was connected to the fact that he needed to convince all these "dust people" that God was the one judging Job. So, this is a very special case, and considering the fact that this story documents "oppression" instead of "possession," we can learn much about the abilities of spirits as they relate to Job's life!

In my life, I've had dozens of accounts of dealing with demons, although I didn't know it at those times. There was a time when I was sleeping, and a demon stuck its upper face into my forehead. I was able to see its face in the darkness of my mind with my "mind's eye," if there is such a thing. I said in my mind, "In the name of Jesus, I command you to leave!" It backed off quickly! If I were a good artist, I'd be able to draw it. That brownish, rotten-looking skin and those hollow, pitch black spaces for eyes staring at me is something I'll never forget! I consider this as a memory instead of a dream because I do not know how to lucid-dream; I do not know how to control dreams while I sleep, yet that one and only time I happened to control the demon with my words of my thoughts. What this memory tells me now as I look back on it is that demons have the ability to spy on the inside of your body. They try to sneak peaks inside you to see how your brain works, to see if there's any mindset inside that gives them a right to stick around you. They can only stay if something invites them. (I will prove this later in the chapter.) They peer. They watch. They listen when you talk in general to wait for legal invitations in your words through vows that you speak.

It's important to note in this instance that I was a

younger child when this happened to me. I had not learned about forgiveness through Jesus Christ yet, although I was taught about God and Jesus in general. So, the act of demons peering into a person who is a nonbeliever versus being able to peer into believers is still up to debate inside me. I became a confessing Christian at age 13, and I am now able to understand differences of demonic activity after the fact as opposed to before I was saved.

More examples ensued from my childhood into adulthood. I've been tormented in my dreams before with demonic stories of a man biting off his own arms. One time, something decided to wake me up by knocking on the inside of my skull. I've had YEARS of dealing with sleepless nights. I'd hear voices of ridicule and shame broadcasted onto me while I was trying to sleep sometimes. One "woman" said about me while I was half asleep, "Even HE doesn't really believe! HAHAHA" These things are all lies. I know it, but I didn't always know it. There were times I had been attacked while I had been receiving the Words of the Day in 2020; the tinnitus in my head that I've been used to for years became unbearable. Other attacks included having to fight my hand from stabbing me in the eye with a pen! And at a couple of key points, I was told to kill myself. The devil was ANGRY at the grace that God was teaching me in this book! Lots of times since my early adult years, I'd "have" a thought and I thought that I was the one thinking it. Sometimes they were blasphemous words against God. As it is clear in Job chapter 4, devils do not have to enter inside a body in order to do damage to us or affect us. Their lies do enough damage socially and spiritually. They are always looking for ways to speak to you and convince you that you are the one thinking evil thoughts!

So, does this mean that I'm saying that all the depictions

in cartoons of angels and demons hovering over people's shoulders, whispering into the characters' ears to convince them to do good or evil, is basically true? ...Yes, to a point. Angels of God don't need to "convince" people of anything, especially when the Holy Spirit dwells inside Christians, acting as their voice of leading. Angels simply do as the Lord commands, like protect people. So, devils are really the only ones on people's shoulders, trying to weigh them down with negative words and feelings. The Accuser is no longer in heaven next to the Father, accusing mankind to God concerning all their deeds, day in and day out. The only thing the devil has left that he is capable of doing is to directly accuse each human of their sins, to convince each human to condemn himself/herself away from the belief and saving grace of the Father through Christ Jesus. (Revelation 12:5+9-10 is part of the backstory that is displayed to John in a vision. Based on the timeline of the representative events, it shows that Satan was cast out of heaven after Christ had performed the work of the cross. Verse 5: "And she [Israel] brought forth a man child, who was to rule all nations with a rod of iron: and her child was caught up unto God, and to his throne." I encourage you to read all of Revelation 12 for context. After Jesus was caught up to the throne of God, there was a war in heaven between the angels and the demons. Verses 9+10: "And the great dragon was cast out, that old serpent, called the Devil, and Satan, which deceiveth the whole world: he was cast out into the earth, and his angels were cast out with him. And I heard a loud voice saying in heaven, Now is come salvation, and strength, and the kingdom of our God, and the power of his Christ: for the accuser of our brethren is cast down, which accused them before our God day and night.") The backstory in Revelation 12 gives good insight into why Satan was able to visit God in the congregation of angels in heaven, and it also shows that Satan was allowed to travel between the realms of heaven and earth, as he did already when he visited Adam and Eve to temp them into sin, as well as the time when the evil spirit visited Eliphaz. In the very story about Job, Satan accuses Job in front of God of not being as perfect as God said he was. At the end of their conversation, God asserts his dominance by saying in chapter 1 verse 12, "only upon himself put not forth thine hand," but I argue that God's phrase beforehand of, "Behold, all that he hath is in thy power," was not a declaration of permission, but a declaration of the authority that Satan already possessed when he convinced Adam and Eve to sin. (Refer to 2 Corinthians 4:4 as it describes Satan as "the god of this world.") It was like saying, "Satan, you already have the power to do this, so why ask? But since you're talking about affecting Job's life like this, I'm telling you right now that I don't want you to touch him directly." This whole transaction of words feels ridiculous and unnecessary, but Adam transferring his authority of the earth to Satan was also ridiculous and unnecessary! I can only imagine how annoyed God was, having to obey his own law by listening to Satan's petitions against people God loved!

So, I've laid out the groundwork of understanding that Satan and his demons make it a point to convince human beings to sabotage their own lives. Let's consider some verses and reasoning, explaining as to why this is the demons' method of choice.

Proverbs 18:21: "Death and life are in the power of the tongue: and they that love it shall eat the fruit thereof." Eating the fruit of your words means that you become what you say and reap those words' consequences.

Luke 6:43-45: "For a good tree bringeth not forth corrupt fruit; neither doth a corrupt tree bring forth good fruit. For every tree is known by his own fruit. For of thorns men do not gather figs, nor of a bramble bush gather they grapes. A good man out of the good treasure of his heart bringeth forth that which is good; and an evil man out of the evil treasure of his heart bringeth forth that which is evil: for of the abundance of the heart his mouth speaketh." These verses in Luke further clarify that the FRUIT people produce by what they speak really comes from what is inside their hearts, basically put, what they choose to believe or their mindsets. What you believe is what you become.

So, how do you come to the point of choosing what to believe and speak in order to create an intended reality? It's all based off what you hear and absorb through learning. We are empty vessels as children, filled as products of our environment until we finally learn the truth in Christ, in which case, we then become enemies of this worldly environment.

Romans 10:17: "So then faith cometh by hearing, and hearing by the word of God."

Jesus answers his disciples' question about why they couldn't cast out a demon in Matthew 17:20, as I've mentioned before. "And Jesus said unto them, Because of your unbelief: for verily I say unto you, If ye have faith as a grain of mustard seed, ye shall say unto this mountain, Remove hence to yonder place; and it shall remove; and nothing shall be impossible unto you."

In Matthew 17:20, Jesus literally equates "belief" with "faith." So, although Romans 10:17 is talking about receiving belief of the word of God through hearing, we can deduce that whatever you hear and feed your spirit-man affects what you believe and say as well because you can hear evil things and choose to have faith in those negative thoughts! Let's look at the logic behind belief. In life, we receive information all the time, every day, 24/7. Our bodies' senses are part of what speaks to our inner beings. Whenever we receive a piece of information, we are automatically faced with a decision. We must choose if we believe what we're experiencing or not. Then we must make a decision concerning our responses thereafter. There are no choices in life other than "yes," "no," and "maybe." I feel that it is a common fact that those who "walk by the flesh" as opposed to "walking by the Spirit" will automatically believe whatever their senses tell them.

Here's a pictorial example of this understanding concerning always being in the position of choosing what to believe. You're walking down the street, and you suddenly see a hat levitating on the sidewalk across the street. It baffles you because it defies what you originally learned about the world of physics. When you learned about physics, you automatically believed what you learned because you were a blank slate as a child. You learned physics based on what your senses told you as well as what people told you. You have a few choices: disbelieve what you saw; believe that you saw the hat levitate, but don't believe how it happened; believe that it happened without doubt or investigating the cause. When you don't believe, that's it. You've made a choice, and it doesn't need to be researched any further. When you believe what you saw but don't like how it contradicts what you previously understood as truth, it's like answering "maybe" to a yes/no question. You have to go find out more information because you've chosen that it will bother you. (Most people fall under this "No-for-now" category that "maybe" represents.) Upon further investigation, you find that the hat was on top of a vent blowing air. Your previous beliefs of your knowledge of physics have now been reinforced, and you are at peace. Of course, we could just have faith like children and automatically believe, instead, without needing to investigate why it happened, but is that always wise?

Matthew 14:22-33 is a good story about faith in this regard. Jesus walks on the water to meet the disciples on the ship, and Peter asks to walk to him out on the water. Peter kept his eyes on Jesus; that is how he retained the faith that he could walk on water as well, after Jesus had said the word that he could walk out to him. Once he turned his attention to the waves and wind, his carnal beliefs remembered, "Wait a second! I'm supposed to be sinking right now!" And he did just that. Jesus had to pull him up so that they could both walk to the ship.

When we consider Job 4, how Eliphaz responded to the spirit, he didn't make a choice to disbelieve it. He didn't make a choice to question the validity of what the spirit said. He, in fact, received its words with blind faith. The words probably weren't far off from what he already believed, considering how all the friends followed along to accuse Job with what they already similarly believed as well. The next 30-or-so chapters of accusations were most likely derived from a common set of beliefs between the friends. The fact that Eliphaz received the words from a spirit probably empowered him to boldly accuse Job as if he were correct. But as we can see, from whom you receive information is extremely important. This spirit was bad news!

I can attest in my own life that demons have been talking to me since I was little. They've been filling my head with lies like it was their full-time job! As a child, I suffered from "bipolar with racing thoughts." These random thoughts caused me to have impulses, through which it was like my body made a decision concerning an action without thinking the action through. I felt violent. I felt suicidal.

Nobody would have ever known because the self-condemnation and shame I carried made me feel like I was supposed to maintain a good persona around everyone in order to have worth and life purpose. My self-control was uncanny because people's opinions about me were more important than carrying out a random thought about punching someone, sexually harassing someone, or hurting myself. Come to find out that the mindsets I carried concerning self-condemnation and shame of what I thought were MY wrongdoings were also suggestions I unknowingly received from spirits and did not validate, accepting with blind faith that I was unlovable.

This didn't start to change until I heard God's voice on a day that I had accepted to kill myself, when I was 13. He said, "Stephen, if you do not choose me, you shall surely die." When God interacts, the truth of it is undeniable. My body felt numb. The air was thick. I could almost see the air move. I heard the words of my thoughts being played like an instrument when he said this. It was after this moment that I knew God was real, and that I had to search for him. It's been about 20 years now!

As I write this now, God's revealing in me that the reason he talked to me in that way from outside my body was to show the truth about how demons talked to me, except that God doesn't lie to me about who he is, while the demons make it a point to hide their identities behind their "instrument-playing," strumming the electrical impulses of my brain like guitar strings, in a way, controlling my body like a marionette with the power of suggestion. If a doctor can use a tiny hammer to hit your knee to make your leg twitch, I have no doubt that they can "twitch" other parts of the body! They also want us to believe that WE are the ones thinking these negative thoughts and choosing these physical actions. If we believe that we are the ones thinking these suggestions, we'll be more apt to agreeing with the thoughts. When we believe and agree with the thoughts, we have then chosen to make them a part of who we are.

I remember a time I was receiving a doctrine from someone concerning whether Mary, the mother of Jesus, was a virgin or not. It was a far-out idea. The biblical references were shaking me, though, and then suddenly I received a thought in my head that said, "If this is true, I'm going to deny Christ!" I started crying and pleading with God, saying, "God, I would never deny you! That thought wasn't from me, and I refuse to accept that thought!" After crying and praying a little longer, I suddenly received a peace flow from inside me. My body started to tingle and become numb, and then I heard God say to me in my thoughts, "You know who I AM." When God moves your spirit, you know it!

It is because of things like this that I have begun to believe that demons most often try to implant their suggestions by talking to us or strumming our brains FROM THE OUTSIDE to make us FEEL things. When you live any part of your life based in the flesh instead of the Spirit, it's very easy to be controlled because the flesh considers evil suggestions to be like wisdom. I'm able to see the lies now because God has filled my life with his truths and helps me to live through his Spirit. Also, I can now tell the difference from where these thoughts originate. When God manifests spoken words into my thoughts, it is a feeling that is welled up from inside of me. When I hear and feel things from demons, it is always from the outside of my body. I know what God is about to say from inside of me before he voices it, whereas demons try to leave me in confusion with their words, feelings, and thoughts.

One time in the middle of a cloudy night, I was outside

my house, talking to my friend about the truths of the universe (the questions that I asked God concerning the nature of the universe of which I referenced in the Sermon About Faith). At one point, I heard quick stomping footsteps running towards my right side very close to me. I looked, but nothing was there in the open clearing of the field. My friend asked me what happened because he saw my reaction but didn't hear the footsteps, and while I was answering him, the right side of my face felt numb with a pressure against it, and I was receiving feelings of artificial sadness. I said, "A demon is annoyed at what I'm telling you and is trying to distract me and make me afraid. 'In the name of Jesus, leave me alone.'" I felt my face again, and the feelings of sadness were gone.

A different time, I had been called to my friend's house to cast out demons from occupying a space. It was a strange situation in which I found myself because I wasn't exactly sure what to do. I simply followed the Holy Spirit's leading. I went to each room of the house and blessed them, calling angels to protect each room and casting roaming demons away from each room. As I was in the basement, praying over the main room, my forehead felt numb, and I received the thought, "Do you realize how stupid you look right now?" This thing didn't even bother to disguise the thought in order to trick me into thinking that it was my thought! I disregarded it and remembered a time when God talked to me, what that felt like, holding onto and using that memory to recall the faith I have in Jesus, much like Peter had when he kept his eyes on Jesus in the water. I carried on with blessing the house. A day later, I learned that my other friend's father had passed away. I was stricken with grief for my friend. Throughout that week, I started feeling worse, like a horrible person for not getting to be there for my friend because I was on a road trip. I ended up also feeling dangerously suicidal for no reason. It's against who I am to hate myself that much again, and yet, I had to emotionally stop myself from jumping off a gondola high up in the air. After a while, I eventually got to meet with my friend and have a talk with him about his father. It was a heart-healing conversation. A week later, I was taking an hour-long drive for business. I had a lot more peace at that point because I wasn't agreeing with the lie of a belief that I'm a bad friend (of which, I believe the demon had taken as an invitation to harass me). Suddenly, though, while I was driving, I felt like I was being stared at. I looked in the direction of the front passenger seat, and I could sense an evil presence. Judging by the feeling, I'm quite certain it was the same demon from the first friend's house. It was invisible, but I could see molecules in the air bouncing off of it. This is how I describe "seeing air move" when a spirit is around me. I opened the window and said, "In the name of Jesus, I command you to leave me alone and leave this car." The presence was gone immediately. I wish that I had cast it into the pit of hell, though!

My experiences seem almost endless, so I will try to focus on just the experiences which relate to scripture and things that God had told me. This experience happened at a couple of sermons on a particular Sunday and Monday; I learned more about focusing on the best gifts from the Holy Spirit. During the sermon, I realized that I didn't know which gifts casting out demons falls under concerning the gifts of the Holy Spirit. I asked God if it falls under the gift of miracles. He kind of disregarded the question, now that I think about it, although I deduce that the gift of miracles is the only logical gift that casting them out falls under. The spiritual feelings I received in response were as follows:

"Demons are not worth mentioning. They are so powerless and insignificant that they do not need to be given a platform to respond. They have been defeated by Christ on the cross! My children need to have the faith of Christ in order to become righteous, before being capable of repelling sinful mindsets. How can my children expect to master delivering people from demons before they master their identity through the enhancement of the gifts of my Holy Spirit and seeking my face first? I have declared, IF MY PEOPLE turn away from their wicked ways and seek my face, I WILL HEAL THEM."

Because of this experience, something very specific was revealed and reenforced inside of me concerning when things relate to demons. "The Old Covenant is different than the New Covenant." When Jesus was casting out demons from people for 2/3 of his ministry, no matter who they were, the dynamic of the power of demons was a lot stronger before Christ was crucified because mankind was still under the Old Covenant where the Accuser had not left God's presence, accusing the world of its sins, and the Holy Spirit had not made his habitation inside man yet. There was nothing stopping a demon from entering a religious Jew if the correct invitations were presented. In fact, as I had mentioned earlier in a previous section, referencing Mark 9:25, if Jesus had to command the dumb and deaf spirit to leave "and enter no more into him," that showed that demons could clearly do whatever they wanted during the Old Covenant era. Otherwise, why would Jesus have to take that extra step to ensure that the demon did not return to possess again? But Praise be to God that Jesus makes demons powerless in his presence inside us now!

During the sermon I attended the next day on Yom

Kippur, when I was learning about the gifts of the Holy Spirit in more detail, I asked God to fill me with his Holy Spirit and anoint me with power in my purpose in his kingdom. He responded, "You are already anointed because you have Christ. He is anointed. You just had to come into full agreement with him. You are already filled with my Holy Ghost. You just have to agree with me in full belief...The way you get filled with my Spirit and receive my power is to just REST IN ME."

God is making it perfectly clear to me that the lack of renewing of the mind into obeying God is the invitation that draws demons close to influence us because the renewing of the mind into unwavering faith and agreement with the truth of Christ pushes ALL evil away from our identity. (God is truth. Everything that is contrary to God is based off of lies.) This is why Christians have been experiencing freedom through the act of denouncing evil from their lives during what I call "mindset deliverance" when we were first learning about the Blue and Green cards and even now as we've learned more about systematic deliverance. (I will explain the significance of the Blue and Green cards in the next chapter.)

I've talked about a lot of experiences already. In this chapter, I need to make the following arguments:

Demons gain invitation to AFFECT any person's life because they stand upon the false mindsets people have (therefore the demons will always be around them, affecting them, weighing them down, even when the people visit a holy place like a church gathering); that the ways that demons affect people are based on whether they have the Holy Spirit inside them or not (non-Christians can be fully possessed while Christians can ONLY be coerced through the powers of suggestion from the outside by impartation of thoughts, voices, images, and false feelings that make people impulsively react if they are operating in the flesh and not centered on God's Spirit); and that not all diseases are caused by demons (but through the authority and power of Christ, we should be able to heal illnesses anyway).

I'll start with the easy topic to handle from the list above: illnesses.

Luke 9:1: "Then he called his twelve disciples together, and gave them power and authority over all devils, and to cure diseases." The fact that this verse says "power and authority over all devils" and "to cure diseases" as two separate phrases logically suggests that these are two separate types of afflictions, meaning that a demon does not have to be present for the body to experience disease. Otherwise, the meaning of the verse would read, "...power and authority over all devils and the diseases they cause." We need God's discernment to know if certain illnesses are caused by demons, like Job had experienced, referencing Job chapter 2.

Next, I need to prove that the ways demons affect people highly depend on whether they have the Holy Spirit or not.

BID Ministries has a very compelling argument towards the fact that even Christians can have demons dwelling inside the flesh, making a parallel between verses like 1 Corinthians 6:19 and the fact that the outer courts of the Old Testament Temple (which represents the "flesh" in the above verse) had plenty of instances where demonic activities were invited to happen there, while the Holy of Holies (which represents where the Holy Spirit dwells in us) remained untouched by sin. This is a great correlation, but the problem with this doctrine is that it needs to provide proof that the parallel of what was happening in the Old Testament Temple is synonymous with what is ALLOWED to happen in the bodies of believers after Christ was resurrected. There are no verses that connect the two and say that the resurrection of Christ does NOT take care of Old Testament curses, while there are other verses that say that Christians are born again and made into new creatures, for example. Also, this parallel of using the Old Testament Temple as a description of how the body is a temple that can be invaded by demons in the same way can only be attributed to the people of the Old Covenant because Christ had not yet stripped the power of demons' dominion over the earth by dying on the cross. Matthew 28:18 "And Jesus came and spake unto them, saying, All power is given unto me in heaven and in earth." This verse before Jesus gives the Great Commission shows the instance that it is proven to us that Jesus gained power of authority over heaven and earth. Therefore, now that we are part of the New Covenant, only those who will be judged by the Old Covenant laws (non-believers of Christ) are subject to be invaded by demons. As I referenced, 2 Corinthians 4:4 says that the devil is this the god of this (fleshly) world.

In order to apply their "temple parallel," the BIDM doctrine needs to disprove all of 2 Corinthians chapter 5 and supporting scriptures, as they pertain to Jesus receiving authority over all of heaven and earth, as well as the fact that demons can no longer dwell inside a vessel in which Christ attains authority. Some key examples to disprove are verses 4, 5, and 17, but I encourage you to read the whole chapter for context.

2 Corinthians 5:4: "For we that are in this tabernacle [human bodies] do groan, being burdened: not for that we

would be unclothed, but clothed upon, that mortality might be swallowed up of life." This verse describes the sin that is left in the mortality of human flesh which is described in Romans 7:9-25 as sinful carnality. In Romans 7:9, Paul is particularly starting to recall a time in his past as an example for his point concerning lingering sin in his flesh. In Romans 7:14, he describes that past self as "carnal, sold under sin." (The fact that he says this but mentions at the end of the chapter that Christ saved him from this, tells me that struggling with the sin of the flesh was a past-tense experience.) Throughout the Romans references, the sin in this carnal flesh is warring with the Spirit. Sin creates death which is mortality, hence why I equate mortality with carnality because Romans 8:6 says, "For to be carnally minded is death; but to be spiritually minded is life and peace."

Furthermore, in Romans 7:24-25a, Paul states a tongue-in-cheek question of which he already knows the answer, stating, "O wretched man that I am! who shall DELIVER me from the body of this death?" The "body of this death" is the lingering sin that inhabits the flesh that he just spent all of Romans chapter 7 describing. Then in verse 25a, he answers, "I thank God through Jesus Christ our Lord." God, through Jesus Christ, is the one who delivers those who choose to believe in him, from the body of death. Verse 25b, "So then with the mind I myself serve the law of God; but with the flesh the law of sin." This verse is the introduction to Chapter 8 which describes HOW God delivers believers: giving us his Spirit so that we might operate in the Spirit and not in the flesh.

2 Corinthians 5:5: "Now he that hath wrought us for the selfsame thing is God, who also hath given unto us the earnest of the Spirit." "The selfsame thing" refers to the end of 2 Corinthians 5:4, "that mortality might be

swallowed up of life." That's the purpose of what he has accomplished through Christ. "Hath given unto us the earnest of the Spirit," means the "pledge" or "transaction" of his Spirit into us. So, verse 5 can be read, "Now he who has caused mortality in us to be swallowed up by life is God, who has also promised his Spirit to us."

The logic I want to raise in this is that deliverance from the "body of death" happens while our spirits are still residing inside these carnal, mortal bodies that will die. As described in Romans chapter 8 and 2 Corinthians 5:5, having a mind that operates in the Spirit (who resides in believers) is how believers are delivered. So, that leads my point into 2 Corinthians 5:17. "Therefore if any man be IN Christ [as one who has let God renew his mind], he is a new creature: old things are passed away; behold, ALL things are become new." Notice how verse 17 says ALL THINGS are become new in these new-believing creatures? "All things" HAS to include the body of this creature along with the spirit. ALSO, notice how it says, "if any man be IN Christ." This explains how "old things are passed away," including one's old mindsets that would cause a Christian to walk out their decisions through the flesh instead of the Spirit. It is the baptism of the Holy Spirit, as we can read in references like 1 Corinthians 12:13, Galatians 3:27, and Matthew 3:11. The order of which it works is that we decide to believe in Christ, receive the Holy Spirit into our bodies, our spirits reside IN the Holy Spirit (imagine being dunked in a pool and kept under indefinitely, but in a good way), and the Holy Spirit resides inside the body, leading us in relationship to daily renew our minds into the obedience of Christ so that we as Christians will never be led by the world to deny Christ.

Moving along, if the body still eventually dies of old age, in which way has it been made new? Let's figure that out!

Romans 8:11: "But if the Spirit of him that raised up Jesus from the dead dwell in you, he that raised up Christ from the dead shall also quicken your mortal bodies by his Spirit that dwelleth in you." "Quicken your mortal bodies" means "to make alive." The verse beforehand says, "And if Christ be in you, the body is dead because of sin; but the Spirit is life because of righteousness." So, when verse 11 says that our mortal bodies will be made alive, it is talking about how the Spirit makes all things new. Even though our bodies carry sin and death which is the sacrifice of our Nazarene Vow to God, I argue that eternal life is RIGHT NOW if you KNOW God the Father and Jesus Christ (both made manifest as the Holy Spirit inside us). John 17:3 says, "And this is life eternal, that they might know thee the only true God, and Jesus Christ, whom thou hast sent."

So, the purpose of the Spirit living in us is so that we can know God personally and that we are able to fulfill what Romans 6:11-13 tells us to do. "Likewise reckon ye also yourselves to be dead indeed unto sin, but alive unto God through Jesus Christ our Lord. Let not sin therefore REIGN in your mortal body, that ye should obey it in the lusts thereof. Neither yield ye your members as instruments of unrighteousness unto sin: but yield yourselves unto God, as those that are alive from the dead, and your members as instruments of righteousness unto God."

How do we not let sin and lust reign in our mortal bodies so that we are delivered? We yield ourselves to the Holy Spirit inside us. In this way, as he makes our spirits alive in his Spirit, so he empowers our bodies to start living for God, and the more that we walk in the renewed mind of living in the Spirit. The Spirit starts to make our bodies already alive and renewed because it is caused to serve God in righteousness as if our bodies are alive. With this victory of the Holy Spirit inside us as we AGREE with his Spirit wholeheartedly, it is impossible for demons to be connected to that which is alive (our flesh) if it is God who makes our bodies alive. For through God IS life! 2 Corinthians 3:17b: "And where the Spirit of the Lord is, there is LIBERTY." True freedom resides wherever LIFE IN CHRIST resides!

Although our physical bodies in this current world will die, they will be made fully glorified when Christ returns. So, THAT is how our mortal bodies can be considered to be made alive by the Spirit of God yet still pass away during this time on earth. The PROMISE of receiving glorified bodies NEGATES the significance that physical death will eventually occur. Therefore, we can agree with Christ in declaring that our mortal bodies are immortal even right now, ACCORDING to that promise! A believer is made into a new creature when he/she is provided the promise of glorification and has been empowered by the Spirit to live righteously, as if we ALREADY HAVE the promised glorified bodies! Case in point, demons cannot be connected to that which has been made truly alive by the Holy Spirit because when we receive the indwelling of the Holy Spirit, we are then returned to our originally created status, eternal communion with God and without sin or death. To fortify this, we see in John 11:25-26 that Jesus considers those who believe in him as those who will NEVER die. "Jesus said unto her, I am the resurrection, and the life: he that believeth in me, though he were dead, yet shall he live: And whosoever liveth **and** believeth **in** me shall **never** die."

Now finally, with the previous point in mind, I must prove biblically that demons gain invitation to AFFECT any person's life based on the false mindsets they possess. ALL mindsets that people possess are gained through what people decide to believe from what is told to them (as I had supported biblically near the beginning of this chapter). What is told to us comes from our human and spiritual senses, what people tell us, what demons tell us, and from what God tells us. Proving that demons gain invitation to possess a non-Christian and annoy Christians from the outside must be done in steps. This section is supposed to be an explanation as to why people of all walks of life can end up being flailed around by a demon during deliverance, whether the demon is inside or outside the body.

Step 1: find out what relationship a demon has with a certain mindset. There are multiple examples to consider. First of all, all demons are lying spirits. If God is truth (John 14:6; 16:13), that means that anyone who opposes God is a liar, and everything that is purposed to oppose God is based in a lie. (I may have repeated this same idea ten times already throughout the book. IT'S IMPERRATIVE THAT YOU UNDERSTAND THAT STANDING IN LIES MAKES YOU VULNERABLE!) This includes all mindsets that oppose God's character. This is why we can't particularly trust what demons say during deliverances. Their whole point of any responses they give would be to distract and confuse us from the truth. (John 8:44: Ye are of your father the devil, and the lusts of your father ye will do. He was a murderer from the beginning, and abode not in the truth, because there is no truth in him. When he speaketh a lie, he speaketh of his own: for he is a liar, and the father of it.) Good examples I previously mentioned of a demon being a liar is when Satan tricked Eve into eating the fruit from the tree and when Satan floated over Eliphaz to empower him to accuse Job. Both times, Satan used half-truths to oppose God, twisting God's words on all occasions.

Concerning other ways of finding how demons are

connected to certain mindsets, I have found in studies that the NAME of a person, place, or thing usually is attributed to an action that is related to him/her/it. Many names in the Bible are evident of this. Moses means, "To draw out of the water," which is what happened to him as an infant.[23] Saul means, "ask for/pray for," which ironically is what Israel did when they asked for a king, and he was the first.[24] Looking up the name Sherah, it means, "fleshly relationship," which signifies that this person was good at dealing with people.[25] The Sherah in the Bible ended up building two cities, of which she'd need to convince many people to follow her in this action. (1 Chronicles 7:24) The demon who went by the name "Legion" was simply a collection of a legion of demons in one vessel. This pattern also follows a lot of names of places after certain battles occurred. Etc.

So how does a demon's name teach us to which mindsets it likes to connect? We can attribute its name to what it does. "Satan" means, "one who is opposed."[26] In order to be in opposition towards something, we can deduce that mindsets of pride, hate, lying, and condemnation are present. So those are mindsets of which Satan specializes. The spirit of divination is focused on divining the future in order to spread confusion and to try to teach people that they don't need God but can rely on their own senses. The spirit of Jezebel is involved with manipulation, idol worship, and all manner of sexual perversion. We can see these traits in the Bible character, Jezebel, the wife of King Ahab, and compare them to mindsets of those who are delivered today from the "spirit of Jezebel." The spirit of Ahab connects to mindsets of laziness and man-pleasing because we can see these traits in the Ahab of the Bible. It's important to note that when demons answer to the names of "Jezebel" and "Ahab," these are not the ACTUAL HUMAN SPIRITS of JEZEBEL AND AHAB; these demons are lying in order to get you to believe in something false. Jezebel and Ahab were evil humans who will be judged in the last days. These human spirits are not multiplying to inhabit the bodies of other humans all over the world for thousands of years. But still, take note if the demons go by these names because it usually describes what mindsets the hosts have that has invited these demons inside or near their bodies.

The same is understood of the demon, Lilith. Folklore in the 1500s describes Lilith as the second human made from the dust at the same time as Adam, before Eve was made. She (supposedly...not) ended up defying God and Adam, and Satan took her "under his wing" so that she would become a demon. She's said to be a succubus demon who rapes men and births Nephilim. She is invited through occult practices of witchcraft... As crazy and illegitimate as it sounded reading about Lilith here, we should treat a demon during a deliverance who goes by this name with the same disregard. We will not be fooled into believing false, unbiblical stories, but treat the demon accordingly in the authority of Christ!

Step 2: biblical references where evil mindsets and beliefs invite demons. One of the best examples I can see where mindsets invite demons is Judas Iscariot. When we compare the stories of Judas found in all four gospels, we get a complete picture of what leads up to Satan affecting Judas to betray Jesus. Matthew 26:6-16 and Mark 14:3-10 both describe "indignation" being present in the disciples once Mary broke the box of expensive perfume to anoint Jesus' head and feet, that they murmured amongst themselves about how much money she just wasted that could have been given to the poor.

John 12:1-8 tells the same story, except that Judas was

pinpointed as being the instigator of the anger towards Mary. Verse 6 is extremely important in understanding the mindset Judas had before deciding to betray Jesus. "This he said, not that he cared for the poor; but because he was a thief, and had the bag, and bare what was put therein."

John 6:64 also gives us a hint that those who would betray Jesus had a mindset that didn't believe in him. "But there are some of you that believe not. For Jesus knew from the beginning who they were that believed not, and who should betray him." Not believing in truth, being a thief and a liar, sets Judas up to be used by Satan. Reading all of John chapter 13 draws a bigger picture of this happening. Verse 2 describes Satan affecting Judas with thoughts and feelings fueled by his anger for not being able to cash in on the box of expensive perfume. "And supper being ended, the devil having now put into the heart of Judas Iscariot, Simon's son, to betray him;" The "heart" most commonly describes a person's thoughts, feelings, and emotions. Putting something "into the heart" is an exact depiction of being tempted with the ideas and suggestions of such. Throughout the chapter, they finished eating, and Jesus was washing the feet of all the disciples, including Judas. While he was doing this, he mentioned that he would be betrayed by one of them. The disciples begged to know who it was. Talking in riddles, Jesus said that the one who shared in dipping his bread with him is the one, that Jesus would dip and give the "sop" to him who would betray him. John 13:26-27: "Jesus answered, He it is, to whom I shall give a sop, when I have dipped it. And when he had dipped the sop, he gave it to Judas Iscariot, the son of Simon. And after the sop Satan entered into him. Then said Jesus unto him, That thou doest, do quickly."

Keep in mind, when Judas was receiving thoughts that

he should betray Jesus, they were only inclinations, temptations. Once Judas understood that he was actually going to betray Jesus, he believed in that mindset that he was receiving from Satan. As we can see, Satan had legal rights and permission to enter into Judas, the son of perdition, the man who didn't believe in Jesus.

Luke 22:1-6 highlights the end of the story, where it's reconfirmed in verse 3 that Satan had already entered into Judas when he communed with the chief priests and scribes.

Matthew 26:15 does a very good job at catching the emotion to which Satan was connected in Judas. "And said unto them, What will ye give me, and I will deliver him unto you? And they covenanted with him for thirty pieces of silver." Judas had the love of money and was fueled by greed. Satan took what was already there in his heart as an invitation to enter him, making Judas do his bidding of betraying Jesus.

Step 3: show biblical proof that demons have the ability to control people through the power of suggestion, based on the mindsets. The story of Judas is already a great example of being influenced by Satan on the outside and controlled by Satan from the inside of his body. I now need to show an example of people being CONTROLLED from just the OUTSIDE. 1 Kings chapter 22 tells part of the story of the prophet Michaiah who was summoned to prophesy on behalf of King Ahab. Michaiah always spoke evil of Ahab. Jehoshaphat and Ahab were deciding whether they should go to war against a certain enemy. All of Ahab's prophets told him to go into battle and that the Lord would deliver the victory. When Ahab asked Michaiah, he answered the same way as the other prophets (1 Kings 22:15), but Ahab could tell that he was lying. He basically said, "How many times must I urge you to tell the truth about what God says?" Then Michaiah talks about a conversation God had with his angels in heaven, asking, "Who will convince Ahab to go into battle so that he might fall?" And one angel said, "I will persuade him by being a lying spirit inside the mouths of all his prophets." This became true because even Michaiah stated the lie at first. Some people believe that since this spirit was capable of lying, that it was an unclean spirit who just happened to be in the presence of God and decided to volunteer for the job. I believe that it was an angel who obeyed for God's glory and not against it, in that God wanted to overthrow Ahab's wickedness. Logic suggests that angels and demons have the same abilities but different allowance of power and authority in the world, so whether it was an angel or demon is up for debate.

These prophets who were supposed to hear the words of God were standing around, constantly living it up in the presence of royalty, watching Ahab commit atrocities against the Lord, and they always seemed to prophesy something good to Ahab...they were living a lie and never prophesied the true words of God. This is why I believe that this angel was capable of taking something that already existed in these prophets (their lying mindsets) and planted lies in their mouths through the power of suggestion. The angel didn't possess any of them. What came out of their mouths was what was planted on their hearts by the angel (spoken to their minds directly), of which it agreed with their mindset. It spoke into them, and they blindly believed the words. The reason why Michaiah was able to come to his senses and give a real prophecy was because he didn't live a life of lying. It was not his mindset. So, the angel was powerful enough to put the lie in his mouth, but it could not overcome Michaiah completely.

Everything above is supposed to reveal the smoking gun concerning what happens during deliverances of non-Christians as well as deliverances attempted on Christians. There will be manifestations from both groups, performed in different ways: from within non-Christians; and from the outside of Christians. When a Christian is not living in the complete truth of walking in the Spirit, demons have the legal right to come close and attach themselves to the outside of those Christians, making them feel feelings that are not theirs, speaking thoughts into them based on their mindsets. When a Christian is set free from false mindsets, manifestations can happen just like an angry babysitter shaking a baby...until it finally lets go of the outside of the body. A friend from the Umbrella-Belief Meeting described this very thing happening during an early deliverance session with John and Linda. As he was going through the Blue and Green cards, he was suddenly overtaken by a demon. According to his story, (although he couldn't totally remember this happening, as if he was unconscious) John and Linda witnessed the imprint of a hand around his neck, pushing back and choking him upwards in his seat! We were having this discussion about possessions versus oppressions, and he didn't seem to realize how significant his experience was to my viewpoint in the debate. Demons have the ability to manhandle and afflict the flesh like any other human can punch you in the face! But I digress.

If a Christian speaks falsehoods like, "I need Christ every day because I'm a sinner," the spirit of condemnation is going to hear and take notice of that mindset and say, "I can use that. He doesn't know that he doesn't deserve condemnation since he believes in Christ!" It hovers around him in a heavy manner (most of us know this heavy feeling on our shoulders and being set free from it when we finally believe in truth) and waits for something to happen that it can use to condemn him. The more the spirit of condemnation can keep him in the false mindset with his suggestions, the closer it gets to convincing the Christian to eventually deny Christ if future events can get bad enough for the Christian to give up. This is why it's written, "My people perish for a lack of knowledge." If Christians are not walking in knowledge of their full identity in Christ, they act powerless and allow themselves to be vulnerable. Because of this, they do not overcome the world until the end, eventually denying Christ. This is what makes living as a lukewarm Christian just as dangerous as living as an unbeliever!

When I had my deliverance with Bart and Dylan, the demons that were revealed to me were the spirit of divination (which I thought I had already denounced and had broken agreement, but upon believing what I was told that it must still be in my body, it had the right to hover around me again), Lucifer, Jezebel, and three others of which I can't remember the names. I received answers in my mind to questions Bart and Dylan were asking. I received pictures of people (who were supposedly my ancestors) and stories about how they invited demons into my life through generational curses. These were either the memories of demons, depositing into my mind, or they were false stories. The fact that I am already a very sensitive person makes it very easy for demons to speak to me or deposit thoughts, feelings, and pictures into my mind. One thing I know now, though, biblically and through experiences, is that they are on the outside, and Holy Spirit wells up from the inside. I refuse to let demons make me feel heavy again because I refuse to believe in false mindsets that invite them around me. I choose to live in complete surrendered identity in Christ so that I continue to walk in freedom and that they have nothing on which to stand!

# CHAPTER FOURTY-SIX: LIST OF DEMONIC INFLUENCES

This list has been revised and comprised of examples of demonic influences that can possess non-believers of Christ and oppress Christians from the outside of the body, depending on the invitations that are presented to such demonic influences, based upon the lies to which each individual adheres. This is the doctrine I stick with because I'm convinced that the power and authority of Christ supersedes the capabilities of demons being able to take ownership of bodies and spirits in which the Holy Spirit inhabits. The only thing that is left susceptible to influence by the power of suggestion is the "will" and "emotions" of people, of which this part of the soul can be tempted by the words or emotions given by demons AND/OR by the sin that resides in the flesh. Our wills and emotions are what help us make the choices to accept and follow Christ or accept and follow the whims of rebellion. So, the MIND is THE BATTLEFIELD of sin and demonic influence.

For the following list, the numbered items are the mindsets that represent the "strongmen," and the subcategories are considered as the "underlings." The strongmen are the main cause or supporters of the underlings. Some of the underlings on this list can be used under other strongmen, but for the sake of representation, I formulated the most probable combinations to that of the relationships between strongmen and underling mindsets.

Another thing to understand about the names attached to this list of negative mindsets: names of demons that manifest from a client are useless EXCEPT to give you a hint as to the lie the client believes which gives demonic influence a foothold. Even so, ALL evil spirits are prideful; ALL evil spirits are liars; ALL evil spirits are perverse! If a client starts to manifest uncontrollably, and the demon speaks using the dizzied state and the mouth of the client to say, "I am Jezebel," know FOR SURE that the human spirit of Jezebel, the queen of the evil king Ahab in the time of Elijah, is NOT inside this person or hundreds of thousands of others who have claimed to be possessed by Jezebel! What this tells is that the client probably suffers from addiction and sexual perversion and needs to renounce those false mindsets, habits, traumas, and addictions. Don't throw the "Jezebel" dog a bone by believing the lie that a PERSON is trying to demonically influence you! In this lie, you could be letting it continue to have authority to stick around to continue to lie to you due to agreeing with its fake name. If it wasn't covered enough beforehand, lies are what give demons enough "dough" to knead in order to turn your mind into the "bread" they so desire, a mind that becomes puffed up over time to perform the will of the flesh and sin-nature. The lie concerning a demon's name may seem small and insignificant, but, as an example, when we look at the differences between doctrines that I had previously mentioned involving the "possession versus oppression of Spirit-filled Christians" debate, I concluded that by giving demons authority with a lie in their abilities over your lives, that will allow them to subliminally control you through the power of suggestion. All they have to do is sit on your shoulder, whisper into your ear, and trick you into believing that whatever they are saying is coming from YOU as your own thoughts! Or better yet for them, that the words and feelings you hear are from God! "The greatest trick the Devil ever pulled was convincing the world he didn't exist." - Charles Baudelaire.

So, without further ado, let's go over how to use this list during a "Mind-Renewal Deliverance Session!" The following is influenced by the Blue and Green guidance cards specifically found on the Being Changed Inc. website. [27] You can decide to go to that website to learn how to implement the Blue and Green cards directly, or you can accept my nifty paraphrased instructions I will provide here. The biblical content of that site is not something I have read in complete context in order to 100% agree upon or endorse; everything I know about the cards is based upon what I have experienced firsthand while performing deliverances with John. The process of the cards as used in mindset-deliverance is effective! This is my paraphrased process of the cards:

Below, there are numbered items in the list that represent the "strongmen" that are holding your freedom hostage. For the sake of being thorough, I'll list all of the strongmen below: Pride; Rejection; Unforgiveness; Accusation; Occultism; Sickness; Poverty; and Perversion. In the off-chance that any of these strongmen mindsets exist in a Christian's mind and is giving authority to a demon(s) to torment, based on the particular lie, it's important to BIND the strongmen FIRST. If there is a strongman demon and an underling demon that is there because of the strongman, binding the strongman makes it easier to renounce and pray against the underling. So, the

185

beginning of the deliverance would start off with general prayer in requesting the guidance and discernment from the Holy Spirit. The next part is having the client bind the strongmen in a prayer like this: "In the name of Jesus, I bind the spirit of pride, the spirit of rejection, the spirit of unforgiveness, the spirit of accusation, the spirit of occultism, the spirit of sickness, the spirit of poverty, and the spirit of perversion in my life. Holy Spirit, I pray that you would shield me from these wicked mindsets and demonic forces and hold such spirits from having any authority over my mind." Your prayer doesn't have to be exactly like that, but I thought I'd give you a good example. In fact, on the actual Blue and Green cards, they liked the idea of instructing clients to say, "In the name of Jesus of Nazareth," just to be specific. When the client says this prayer and declares binding of any attached spirits, pay close attention to how the client responds. Typically, if it is very difficult to speak out against a particular spirit, he/she is probably being influenced/oppressed by such a spirit. This will help determine what needs to be surrendered to Christ as the deliverance progresses. Next, the underling spirits of each strongman must be denounced and cast away, the equivalent mindsets to be denounced and cast out from the client's mind. It can be done as follows: "In the name of Jesus Christ, I cast out the mindsets of unbelief, fear, arrogance, hate, violence, murder, discord, envy/jealousy, codependency, laziness, passivity, man-pleasing, addiction, and lust. I cast out abandonment, insecurity, bitterness, resentment, guilt, shame, worthlessness, depression, suicide, condemnation, self-pity, regret. I denounce and cast away all lying spirits, spirits of divination, witchcraft, Molech, and that of idolatry. I denounce and cast away spirits of Shakra worship and Kundalini. I cast out false mindsets of physical illness,

186

mental illness, and any deaf and dumb spirits connected to illness! I cast out the mindsets of unworthiness, self-preservation, and self-righteousness from my life! Father, in the name of Jesus, cast away all conjoining demons and throw them all into the abyss of hell!"

The next step is to cast away the strongmen. (We BOUND the strongmen the first time; this time they go away. Pay attention and keep up!) The understanding here is that if there are any demonic spirits connected to a client's life, the strongmen have less of a hold after any underlings are dispersed. It's the deconstruction of circular reinforcement; a metal pole becomes a lot weaker when it's flattened horizontally by a steamroller. This is another good example: a man wants to stop being a porn addict, but he is also addicted to watching TV screens and social media; if he positively fights the addiction to electronics and media by banishing or limiting them from his life, beating the porn addiction can become much easier. So, after casting away the underlings, the client can now cast the bound strongmen away in the same manner. "Father, in the name of Jesus Christ, I denounce and cast away the spirit of pride, the spirit of rejection, the spirit of unforgiveness, the spirit of accusation, the spirit of occultism, the spirit of sickness, the spirit of poverty, and the spirit of perversion in my life. Banish them to the abyss of hell!" You can also add, "I denounce the sin of the flesh by reaffirming my belief and devotion in Jesus Christ as my Lord and Savior," but as I will mention in the first paragraph of the list, belief in Christ is something that should really happen BEFORE the deliverance of any demons occurs.

The back of the Blue card system involves a guided prayer that helps the client claim responsibility for the lies that he/she believed, how one should have systematically cast out the spirits, asking for forgiveness for letting the spirits into his/her life, breaking generational curses, and finally, asking God to "heal the place where the spirits" had been and to "fill that place with Yourself." My problem with this section of the Blue card is that by stating these things in this order, it's almost like saying that the Holy Spirit was not filling you in the first place. When you believe in Christ as the first step of deliverance, you should have already repented of your sins and asked for general forgiveness, letting Christ be the Lord over your life and filling you with his Holy Spirit. Repenting of newly discovered/committed sins is always a must in reconciling to God in relationship, but that's not the point in this card, as it is repentance for something that was already covered by the blood of the cross. When you receive Christ, you are a new creation and part of a NEW LINEAGE to which generational curses do not belong. (Galatians 3:29 and 4:7) These are simple keys. It's why I resolved to leave out the back side of the Blue card from the above prayer of renouncing evil mindsets/demonic influences. I've said before that deliverance through renewal of the mind is like a blood transfusion. Pushing out the infected blood (lies) must happen simultaneously with injecting good blood (truth). This is why I wrote about identity, faith, and truth through affirmations in the first place in this book before EVER trying to explain deliverance from demons! Going into a deliverance without having understanding in your Christian identity and faith will make you susceptible to more lies from the enemy!

I pray that this list sheds light onto the dark places of your life as you go through this transfusion process! Here's the list to use in the above process:

1. The sin of the flesh

Although the sin of the flesh is not a demon, it is something that we denounce BY accepting Jesus as our

Lord and Savior. Never, and I repeat, NEVER try to cast out demons from a non-Christian. In Matthew 12:43-45 and congruent verses, Jesus had been talking about that current wicked generation and compared it to a man who had been possessed by demons. "When the unclean spirit is gone out of a man, he walketh through dry places, seeking rest, and findeth none. Then he saith, I will return into my house from whence I came out; and when he is come, he findeth it empty, swept, and garnished. Then goeth he, and taketh with himself seven other spirits more wicked than himself, and they enter in and dwell there: and the last state of that man is worse than the first. Even so shall it be also unto this wicked generation." Although this was a comparative statement talking about that wicked generation, this description has become a common warning for those in deliverance ministries, not for the same reasons, though. (I know of no other besides myself who's come to this conclusion of Christians being "oppressed" versus "possessed" and yet still advocates that systematic deliverances are a good thing.) We can tell from these verses that such a possessed man was not one who belonged to God, based off the statement that the hypothetical demon made: "I will return into MY HOUSE from whence I came out." I argue the fact that because it was empty with no Holy Spirit, the empty house (which other verses in the Bible use the term "house" to express as the "physical body") leaves a person wide open to being entered again! A clue that this is even possible in demonstration is something I've mentioned before when Jesus cast out the deaf and dumb spirit in Mark 9:25. "When Jesus saw that the people came running together, he rebuked the foul spirit, saying unto him, Thou dumb and deaf spirit, I charge thee, come out of him, and enter no more into him." I argue that if a demon could not reenter the same person twice, Jesus would not have needed to tell the demon, "enter no more into him." And remember, all the people Jesus preached and healed were under the Old Covenant; nobody under the Old Covenant was able to have the Holy Spirit dwell inside them because Jesus had not yet died on the cross, resurrected, and ascended. Case in point, if you are working with clients who have revealed that they don't believe in Jesus Christ nor want to follow him, stop the rest of the deliverance and concentrate on counseling the clients in the dangers of being delivered as a non-believer as well as helping them understand why they should want to submit to Christ. While Christians are protected from being "housed" by demons, non-Christians are not protected after a deliverance. Keep in mind that if a non-Christian is seeking deliverance, MOST LIKELY demonic torment is involved. The first step should always be accepting the Holy Spirit before anything else happens. He is the key to true freedom and deliverance from evil! This is the simple gospel.

2. Pride (Hillel/Lucifer/Satan)
- Unbelief
- Fear
- Arrogance
- Hate
- Violence, murder, discord
- Envy/jealousy

3. Rejection
- Codependency
- Laziness, passivity, and man-pleasing (Ahab)
- Addiction, Lust, Anger (Jezebel)
- Abandonment
- Insecurity

4. Unforgiveness
- Bitterness
- Resentment
- Guilt
- Shame
- Worthlessness
- Depression
- Suicide
- Condemnation
- Self-pity
- Regret
5. Accusation
- Lying spirit
6. Occultism
- Divination
- Witchcraft
- Idolatry
- Molech
7. Sickness
- Shakra worship/witchcraft
– Kundalini
- Deaf/Dumb spirit
– Mental illness
– Physical illness
8. The spirit of Poverty
- Unworthiness
9. The spirit of Perversion
- Self-preservation
- Self-righteousness (Leviathan)

Everything above in this chapter has to do with the Blue

card system. What usually happens during a deliverance, if the client is honest, is that the Holy Spirit will reveal the evil mindsets or lies in the list above to which he/she believes and needs to let go. Another thing the Holy Spirit will reveal is WHY these mindsets and influences have taken root in the client's mind. Most of the time, such things are caused by traumatizing events which act as "door points" of impartation. A traumatic event can be a door point because it is usually an experience that happens outside the client's control and forces them to believe in something negative. Those who believe that Christians can be possessed by demons believe that these openings allow demons into the body, whereas I believe they simply open a Christian up to the power of suggestion due to the existence of the negative mindset. Either way, trauma can be extremely dangerous if one lets these life events effect what he/she believes is truth. One trauma I keep having to face every so often is the hardship of creating two broken families in the past ten years. I'm reminded of those failed relationships every time I visit with my kids. I love all my children, but the mistakes of the past tend to creep on me and try to convince me that I've failed as a father. I have to constantly be reminded of the truth that my IDENTITY is not to be a "father." My identity is to be a son of God. There is nowhere that I can fail where Jesus hasn't already paid the price for me! Upon surrendering this trauma to him, my health started to improve, and my focus and drive to perform God's will became clearer!

The Green card is structured to handle trauma as a way to close the "door points" of the mind. These are the steps as mentioned on the Being Changed Inc website:

1. Break off the trauma
2. Give the trauma to the Lord
3. Forgive all people involved in the trauma, including

yourself
4. Use the Blue cards to deal with spirits that entered via the trauma
5. Close the door point
6. Pray for God's healing where the trauma had been

I understand that I wrote about the Blue card first and that their system integrates the Blue card in the middle of the Green card, but I have found that by extending the List of Demonic Influences to include so many strongmen and underlings, the Blue card system becomes a strong tool to detect traumas in a client's life, instead of having to "dig" for the traumas so as to reveal them. Essentially, I used the general practice of Bart's BID Ministries with an extended list that is formatted like Being Changed Inc's design. I have found that when I go through this new process with myself, it emulates a process of renewing my mind as well as bringing every thought captive into the obedience of Christ, like 2 Corinthians 10:5 says! It's to the point where once a lie is spoken to me or if I experience a trauma, I don't have to pull out my book in order remind myself to surrender the thought to God. It becomes second nature, a typical, spiritual habit! I DECLARE TO YOU THAT YOU WILL DO THE SAME IN JESUS' NAME!

# FAREWELL

THANK YOU FOR TAKING THE TIME TO READ THIS INSPIRED GIFT FROM THE HOLY SPIRIT! I AM EXTREMELY HONORED AND BLESSED THAT GOD CHOSE ME OF ALL PEOPLE TO EXTEND HIS MESSAGE OF LEARNING THE TRUTH ABOUT IDENTITY, FAITH, AND DELIVERANCE FOUND IN THE BLOOD OF JESUS CHRIST! AS I SAY GOODBYE TO YOU, I WANT TO REMIND YOU (if the whole content of this book hasn't reminded you already) THAT YOU ARE LOVED! YOU ARE SPECIAL TO GOD! YOU ARE WORTH EVERY SECOND IT TOOK TO POUR GOD'S HEART INTO THESE WORDS, AS JESUS POURED HIS BLOOD IN PLACE OF YOURS! IT'S IMPORTANT TO UNDERSTAND THAT ALL HUMANS HAVE ONLY ONE LIFE WITH WHICH TO CHOOSE CHRIST'S FORGIVENESS AND ATONEMENT.

John 3:17-18: "For God sent not his Son into the world to condemn the world; but that the world through him might be saved. He that believeth on him is not condemned: but he that believeth not is condemned already, because he hath not believed in the name of the only begotten Son of God."

FOR THE SAKE OF ESCAPING ETERNAL DAMNATION BECAUSE OF SIN THAT WAS PASSED DOWN THROUGH THE GENERATIONS FROM ADAM, AND FOR THE SAKE OF EXPERIENCING ETERNAL LIFE THROUGH KNOWING CHRIST JESUS AND HIS FATHER (John 17:3), WILL YOU PRAY THIS PRAYER HERE AND NOW IF YOU HAVE NOT ALREADY SUBMITTED YOURSELVES OR IF YOU WANT TO RESUBMIT YOURSELVES TO JESUS AS LORD AND SAVIOR? CONTINUOUSLY CHOOSING CHRIST FOREVER NEEDS TO START FROM SOME POINT, AND RIGHT NOW IS JUST AS GOOD OF A TIME AS ANY! PRAY THIS OUT LOUD:

"Father God, I believe that you are real. I believe that Jesus Christ is your perfect Son who you sent to die in place of my sins that I carry and that you raised him from the dead for my sake. Father, I ask for forgiveness of those sins; I ask that you deliver me from this body of sin and death and turn me into a new creature, spiritually, emotionally, and physically. Lord, please baptize my spirit INTO your HOLY SPIRIT. Work in my heart, Lord, and cause me to become more like Christ every day! Teach me how to renew my mind in you every day! I invite your Holy Spirit into my heart. I invite Jesus into my heart. You are the lover of my soul, and I choose to love you and follow you forever! Thank you, Father. In the name of Jesus, amen."

I love you, brothers and sisters! Welcome to God's kingdom!

# SUPERSCRIPT NOTES AND REFERENCES:

1. Shuttlesworth Jr., Ted. *A Complete Guide to Biblical Fasting.* Ted Shuttlesworth Jr., 2020.
2. Todd White's quote can be found 23 minutes into this full video, but I encourage you to watch the whole thing. It's a wonderful depiction of the gospel! (https://www.youtube.com/watch?v=lK6_MNSqX2s) (Todd White - Gods Heart for Humanity)
3. Reference of the August 21, 2017 solar eclipse that cut the United States in half overhead: https://eclipse2017.nasa.gov/eclipse-who-what-where-when-and-how.
4. June 16, 2020, a massive dust storm blew from the Sahara Desert towards and reaching the Caribbean and some of the shores of Eastern United States: https://www.washingtonpost.com/weather/2020/06/18/sahara-dust-plume
5. Reported as of June 26, 2020, swarms of locusts had plagued many areas in Easter Africa and the Middle East, threatening starvation upon millions of people whose food the locusts had eaten:

https://www.weforum.org/agenda/2020/06/locusts-africa-hunger-famine-covid-19

6. "Charity" https://av1611.com/kjbp/kjv-dictionary/charity.html

7. "harpazo" https://www.blueletterbible.org/lang/lexicon/lexicon.cfm?Strongs=G726&t=KJV

8. "Pleroo" https://www.blueletterbible.org/lang/lexicon/lexicon.cfm?Strongs=G4137&t=KJV

9. "crown" https://www.blueletterbible.org/lang/lexicon/lexicon.cfm?Strongs=G4735&t=KJV

10. "habitation" https://bit.ly/2QXEOiu

11. "habitat" https://bit.ly/3aCnciY

12. "rhema" https://www.blueletterbible.org/lang/lexicon/lexicon.cfm?Strongs=G4487&t=KJV

13. "Shama" https://www.blueletterbible.org/lang/lexicon/lexicon.cfm?Strongs=H8085&t=KJV

14. "afflict" https://bit.ly/3gEe951

15. "Meek" https://bit.ly/2S6pzEo

16. "meekness" https://av1611.com/kjbp/kjv-dictionary/meek.html

17. "talent" https://bit.ly/3vm9OYd

18. "paradigm" https://bit.ly/3sTAMVw

19. "affirmation" https://bit.ly/3ezF3Za

20. Solomon's Temple 3D rendition: https://www.youtube.com/watch?v=y2tha7ogpec

21. "wind" and "spirit" https://www.blueletterbible.org/lang/lexicon/lexicon.cfm?Strongs=G4151&t=KJV

22. Being changed ministries website:

https://beingchanged.com

23. "Moses"
    https://www.blueletterbible.org/lang/lexicon/lexico
    n.cfm?Strongs=H4872&t=KJV

24. "Saul"
    https://www.blueletterbible.org/lang/lexicon/lexico
    n.cfm?Strongs=H7586&t=KJV

25. "Sherah"        https://www.sheknows.com/baby-
    names/name/sherah

26. "Satan"
    https://www.blueletterbible.org/lang/lexicon/lexico
    n.cfm?Strongs=H7854&t=KJV

27. The Blue and Green deliverance cards of the Being
    Changed              Inc.              Ministry:
    https://beingchanged.com/materials/ministry-cards